AF510084

AI - The Code of WHY?

Welcome to the future. It begins with *'WHY.'*

'AI amplifies human potential, but the '***why'*** lies in how we apply its benefits for the greater good.'

...Geoffrey Hinton

'Every great discovery starts with a question. In this book, we explore not just *what* AI is or *how* it works, but '***why***' it matters to you, to society, and to the future of human potential.'

...Simon Sinek

'To decode AI, we must first explore the '***why***' much like understanding the depths of human thought.'

...John McCarthy

The biggest success for any entrepreneur is innovation. You can never, never, never rest on past laurels.

... Shahnaz Hussain

'AI begins with the '***why***' and often, the most unimaginable innovations come from asking the simplest questions.'

...Alan Turing

AI - The Code of WHY?

Unlocking the Purpose Behind Artificial Intelligence

RAJ SINGH

BOOK WRITING INN
UNVEIL YOUR STORY

London, United Kingdom

Author Reflection

When we speak of artificial intelligence, the conversation often begins with what *AI can do and* how *fast it is advancing. Yet the deeper question- the one that defines its true impact - is* why *AI.*

The Code of WHY? is not a philosophical luxury; it is a strategic necessity. The organisations that can answer why *they deploy AI will not only lead in innovation, but also unlock the most* ***sustainable profits and competitive advantage****.*

The future of AI is not about machines replacing humans, but about ***machines amplifying human potential****. This is where profitability lies, not in cost-cutting alone, but in* ***value creation****, new business models, and markets we cannot yet imagine. By asking* why*, leaders can design AI systems that* ***empower employees, delight customers****, and* ***build trust*** *in ways automation alone never could.*

Trust itself will become the ***currency of the AI era****. Customers, regulators, and society will demand more than* *just efficient algorithms they will demand to know* why *a decision was made. Those who can provide that clarity will win loyalty, adoption, and long-term growth. Those who cannot will fade into irrelevance.*

History teaches us a simple truth: the most profitable innovations, the internet, cloud, mobile were not just technical achievements; they were ***answers to a profound "why"****. AI is no different. The leaders of tomorrow will be those who align* ***advanced intelligence with meaningful human needs****.*

This book, **AI – The Code of WHY?** *is my invitation to explore this frontier with you: to decode not only the "*how *of AI", but the* why *that will shape its role in our future our businesses, our societies, and our lives.*

Because the real profit is not in the algorithms. It is in the ***purpose*** *behind them.*

For

My parents — the first teachers of my life.

Guruji — who showed me the true path.

My wife — whose love and guidance keep me grounded.

My daughter — whose innocence and inspiration light my journey.

For,

why we strive.

why we create.

and why we dream.

With love and gratitude,

Raj Singh

Technologist, Innovator, Researcher & Author

This book is a work of non-fiction. The insights, scenarios, and frameworks presented are based on the author's research and practical experience at the frontier of **artificial intelligence and future technologies**.

First Edition: 2025

Published by **@Book Writing Inn**

London, United Kingdom

For permissions, collaborations, or inquiries, please contact:

author@rajsingh.cloud

thecodeofwhy@rajsingh.cloud

www.rajsingh.cloud

About the Author

Technologist | Innovator | Researcher | Author

Mr. Raj Singh is a seasoned technologist with over two decades of experience pioneering advancements across the spectrum of **artificial intelligence, quantum computing, robotics, and technology entrepreneurship**. His career has been defined by a singular pursuit: to decode the intersection of technology and human behaviour, and to transform complexity into clarity.

What distinguishes Raj is his rare ability to **merge technical depth with human-centered storytelling**. He has architected transformative enterprise systems, advanced research in emerging technologies, and authored thought leadership that reframes innovation with purpose. His work consistently reflects a vision where technology is not merely a tool for progress, but a catalyst for **meaning, empowerment, and responsible futures**.

The inspiration for *AI–The Code of WHY?* stems from Raj's lifelong curiosity about **purpose** — the "why" that fuels discovery, invention, and evolution. Devoting nearly a year to research and curation, he has woven together insights that link AI's technical potential with the deeper questions it provokes. This book is not just an exploration of artificial intelligence, but an inquiry into its essence: **why it matters, what it demands of us, and how it can shape tomorrow's possibilities**.

Raj's philosophy — *"AI is Future: Unlock Your Technology Power"* — encapsulates his belief that technology must be an **enabler of creativity, curiosity, and human progress**. Through this work, he seeks to inspire readers to see AI not as a distant algorithmic construct, but as a **partner in reimagining the future of work, society, and innovation itself**.

When not immersed in technological exploration, Raj sketches **futuristic concepts**, engages with diverse cultures to broaden perspective, and mentors the next generation of professionals determined to leave their own mark on the **AI and quantum ecosystem**.

Thank You

This book, AI–The Code of WHY? is more than just words on paper. It is a reflection of the people, love, and guidance that have shaped my life and given me the courage to put my thoughts into the world.

First and foremost, I bow with gratitude to my ***Maa and PitaJi****, who gave me the most precious gift of all – life itself. Their sacrifices, values, and unconditional love are the foundation upon which I stand today.*

To my ***GuruJi****, whose blessings illuminated my path and gave me direction when life seemed uncertain — your wisdom continues to guide me in every step I take.*

To my wife, ***Anchal****, my partner in every sense of the word. Thank you for your endless support, patience, and belief in me, even when I doubted myself. You have been my anchor and my strength. A special thanks for taking such loving care of our daughter while I was deeply immersed in writing. This book would not have been possible without your unwavering dedication and sacrifices. For that, I am forever grateful.*

*To my beautiful daughter, **Tanaisha**, who brings joy, innocence, and a profound sense of purpose into my world. Thank you for making everything real. Your laughter reminds me of love, passion, and the motivation to seek the reason behind The Code of WHY?*

Acknowledgements

Writing **AI–The Code of WHY?** has been both a journey of exploration and reflection. Along the way, I have been fortunate to receive the time, wisdom, and encouragement of many people who generously reviewed my drafts and shared their perspectives.

I would like to extend my sincere gratitude to all the reviewers who engaged with this book - not only for their careful reading but also for their thoughtful feedback. Your comments sharpened my ideas, challenged my assumptions, and helped me make the complex world of AI more accessible and meaningful to readers.

With deep gratitude to **Shahnaz Husain**, Indian entrepreneur, **Founder & CEO**, Shahnaz Herbals Inc., and **Padma Shri** (*one of the highest civilian honours of India-2006*) for lending her voice as a reviewer of this book. Your pioneering work in taking India's Ayurvedic heritage to the world and your insistence on purposeful innovation echo the spirit of *AI – The Code of Why*. Thank you for your time, guidance, and encouragement.

I am especially thankful to my dear friend **Dr Ronan Lee**, Leverhulme Trust Early Career Fellow at **Loughborough University London (UK)**, where he researches the meaning of social vitality for Rohingya refugees. In 2021 he was awarded the ***Early Career Emerging Scholar Prize*** by the International Association of Genocide Scholars. His careful review and plain-spoken guidance pushed me to clarify arguments and keep purpose ahead of scale. Thank you, Ronan, for lending your time and credibility to this work.

With profound gratitude, I thank my brother, **Mr. Rakesh Singh**, Indian **Entrepreneur** & **Spiritual guide (Ramashram Satsang)** with over three decades of wisdom-whose presence has been a steady light on my path. His guidance has grounded me, his counsel has kept me focused on purpose, and his day-to-day support has shaped both my journey and this book. May these pages reflect his enduring lesson: **true progress balances innovation with inner clarity**.

I am equally grateful to my dear friend **Mr. Vinayan William, Founder & CEO** of CoMind, London (UK), whose guidance, encouragement, and strategic insights have been a source of strength throughout this project. I'm deeply grateful for your time, generosity, and belief in this Book.

Special thanks also go to my colleagues, mentors, and friends who gave their time selflessly to critique early chapters, question the "why" behind my arguments, and encourage me to dig deeper into the intersections of technology, ethics, and human purpose.

And finally, to you the reader. Thank you for opening these pages, for sharing your time and curiosity with me. My hope is that this book doesn't just give you answers, but also sparks new questions, awakens wonder, and inspires you to look deeper into the why of the world around us.

This book is stronger, clearer, and more relevant because of your contributions. For that, I remain truly grateful.

The AI- The Code of WHY? is a testament to Raj's unwavering dedication to addressing profound questions and sparking transformative conversations about the 'Why?' behind innovation and the future of technology.

Introduction

In a world that moves at the speed of innovation, we are often left with questions that linger in the background. Questions like 'Why do we need artificial intelligence?' or 'Why is the internet indispensable?' These are not just technological curiosities, but pivotal inquiries that shape how we live, work, and connect.

'WHY?' is a book born from the need to address these questions. It is a journey through the pivotal ***'whys'*** of our time – why we innovate, why we build, why we question, and ultimately, why we strive for progress. Each chapter delves into a specific topic, from AI and robotics to quantum computing and beyond, offering insights that are both profound and accessible.

This book is for the curious, the thinkers, and the dreamers. It is for anyone who has ever looked at the world and wondered about the forces driving its transformation. By exploring the ***'why'*** behind the phenomena that define our age, we not only gain understanding but also the tools to navigate and shape the future.

Through these carefully selected topics, we will dive into the core of innovation, breaking down complex ideas into accessible insights. Whether you're a technology enthusiast, a curious learner, or someone seeking to understand the forces shaping tomorrow, this book invites you to embrace the power of '***why.***'

Let this book be your guide to the 'whys' of our time, sparking curiosity and inspiring action as we explore the fascinating intersections of technology, humanity, and progress.

The Awakening of Inquiry

"The important thing is not to stop questioning. Curiosity has its own reason for existing."

...Albert Einstein

Einstein's reminder about the power of questioning is not just a philosophical reflection, it is a blueprint for human progress. At its core, this quote carries a subtle but profound warning: the day we stop asking **'*why*'** is the day we stop evolving.

In our everyday lives, questions often orbit around the practical. We ask ***what needs*** *to be done* or ***how to get it done***. These are important, but they belong to the surface of existence. The deeper dimension, the one that defines our sense of purpose, begins with the question '***why***'. Why am I doing this? Why does it matter? Why does this path feel right or wrong?

History is a testimony to the power of **'why.'** Every leap of human civilisation, from the invention of the wheel to the discovery of electricity, from space exploration to artificial intelligence, began with someone daring to ask a question that challenged the obvious. The curious few refused to accept life as it appeared; they pushed boundaries by asking what others overlooked.

And now, in the 21st century, as humanity stands at the intersection of biology and technology, intelligence and artificial intelligence, this question of '***why'*** becomes more urgent than ever. Machines are being built to answer questions faster, more accurately, and at scales beyond human capacity. Yet, amidst this abundance of answers, the scarcity lies in meaningful inquiry.

The purpose of this chapter is simple, yet radical: to awaken readers to the forgotten power of *why*. To remind us that behind every algorithm, every business decision, and every personal choice lies a question waiting to be asked. And that, perhaps, is the true code we must uncover in this age of artificial intelligence – ***The Code of WHY?***

Why This Quote Matters in Life?

At the very heart of human progress lies a single force – *curiosity*. Every great invention, every revolution of thought, and every leap of science began not with an answer but, with a *question*. Einstein's words remind us that questioning is not a luxury of philosophers or scientists alone – it is the essence of being human.

In daily life, many of us live in a loop of **'what'** and **'how'**: *What should I do today? How do I solve this task?* Yet very few pause to ask the more fundamental question, ***'Why?'*** Why am I pursuing this path? Why do I follow a system that does not align with my inner values? Why do I continue habits that drain my energy rather than fuel my growth?

The **'why'** is uncomfortable, because it digs into the roots of our existence. It disrupts comfort zones. It forces reflection. But it is only when we dare to ask '***why***' that we awaken to deeper truths. In general life, these awakenings transform passive living into purposeful living.

Why This Quote Matters in the Age of AI?

Artificial Intelligence, at its surface, is a machine's ability to process, learn, and decide. But beneath the algorithms lies a mirror – one that reflects our own patterns of thought and inquiry. If humans simply program machines to answer ***'what'*** and ***'how'*** without ever asking ***'why',*** then AI becomes only an extension of our routines, not a revolution of wisdom.

- **Without Why, AI is a tool.** It calculates, recommends, and automates.
- **With Why, AI is a partner.** It challenges bias, reveals blind spots, and augments human creativity.

For example, consider healthcare. A machine can predict diseases faster than any doctor. But the real question is not ***what disease,*** nor ***how to treat it,*** but ***why*** *did the disease emerge in the first place?* Why do certain communities suffer more than others? Why is prevention neglected while treatment dominates?

Only by programming machines with the spirit of '***why***' can AI help humanity shift from reaction to foresight – from survival to flourishing.

The Philosophical Bridge- Humans, Machines, and Curiosity

Curiosity is not just a biological instinct; it is a bridge between human intelligence and artificial intelligence. A child learns by asking endless **'why'** questions, much like an AI system learns through iterative feedback loops. The difference is that human curiosity is infused with meaning, while machine curiosity (so far) is statistical.

The challenge before us is not simply to build machines that learn, but to design them in a way that they *ask better questions*. If AI can be guided by human values of curiosity, empathy, and responsibility, then the systems we build will not only be powerful – they will be ***purposeful.***

The Awakening in General Life

Applying Einstein's quote in everyday life is not about becoming a philosopher overnight. It is about awakening small moments of inquiry:

- When faced with conflict, instead of asking ***what*** *went wrong?* ask **why** *did this occur at all?*
- When setting goals, instead of asking *how can I achieve more?* ask **why** *do I desire this achievement?*
- When adopting new technologies, instead of asking *what does this tool do?* ask **why** *do I need it in my life?*

This practice of persistent questioning cultivates clarity, resilience, and alignment. It awakens individuals from passive existence and transforms them into architects of their own destiny.

Conclusion – The Code of WHY?

In the age of AI, where answers are abundant and instant, the true scarcity is not ***information,*** but

introspection. The world does not need more tools that answer ***what*** and ***how***. It needs minds human and artificial that persistently ask **'*why*.'**

Einstein's wisdom is not a gentle reminder – it is a call to awaken. To live without questioning is to surrender one's freedom to external forces. To embrace curiosity is to reclaim authorship of life.

'The Code of WHY?' is therefore not just about machines – it is about us. It is about the courage to question, the wisdom to reflect, and the responsibility to guide intelligence – human and artificial – towards a future that is not only smarter, but also more meaningful.

Artificial Intelligence

Welcome to

'THE CODE OF WHY?'

Let the journey begin...

Table of Contents

Acronyms & Glossary

Acronym	Meaning
AI	Artificial Intelligence – Simulation of human intelligence in machines that can learn, reason, and decide.
ANI	Artificial Narrow Intelligence – AI specialised in one task, highly skilled but limited in scope.
AGI	Artificial General Intelligence – Hypothetical AI with human-like cognitive abilities across multiple domains.
ASI	Artificial Super Intelligence – A future state where AI surpasses human intelligence in all fields.
ML	Machine Learning – Algorithms that improve automatically through data experience.
DL	Deep Learning – A branch of ML using neural networks with many layers to analyse complex data.

Acronym	Meaning
RL	Reinforcement Learning – ML approach where systems learn by trial and error to maximise rewards.
NLP	Natural Language Processing – AI's ability to understand, interpret, and generate human language.
XAI	Explainable AI – AI designed to be transparent, interpretable, and explain its decisions.
BCI	Brain–Computer Interface – Direct communication pathway between the human brain and external devices.
IoT	Internet of Things – A network of connected physical devices that share and analyse data.
GPT	Generative Pre-trained Transformer – A model that generates human-like text and creative content.
SBSP	Space-Based Solar Power – Collecting solar energy in space and transmitting it to Earth.

Acronym	Meaning
R&D	Research and Development – Innovation-focused activities to design and improve technologies.
GDP	Gross Domestic Product – The total value of goods and services produced by a country.

Chapter 01

Artificial Intelligence and its Sub-concepts:

1. *Artificial Narrow Intelligence*
2. *Artificial General Intelligence*
3. *Agentic AI*
4. *Artificial Super Intelligence*

What is AI?

Artificial Intelligence (AI)

Artificial Intelligence – often spoken about as if it were magic, machines that ***'think,' 'learn,'*** or ***'decide'*** on their own. But at its heart, AI is profoundly human. It is our curiosity, creativity, and problem-solving instincts expressed through code. It is a mirror of the way we think, distilled into algorithms that can analyse, predict, and act, sometimes faster than we ever could.

Imagine a child learning to recognise faces. At first, they see shapes, colours, and patterns. Over time, with observation and experience, they begin to understand subtle expressions, moods, and intentions. AI works in a similar way. It starts with raw data, numbers, words, images, and through experience, it begins to 'see' patterns, make sense of complexity, and even anticipate outcomes.

Yet AI is not alive, it does not dream, feel, or wonder '***why***' it does, what it does. This is where the human touch becomes essential. While AI can optimise processes, predict trends, and uncover hidden connections, it is humans who must guide its purpose, shape its values, and ask the deeper questions: *Why should this be done? Who benefits from it? And how do we ensure it serves humanity, not just efficiency?*

In essence, AI is both a tool and a companion – a reflection of our own intelligence amplified. It challenges us to think bigger, faster, and smarter. But more importantly, it challenges us to reconnect with the part of ourselves that always asks, always questions, and always seeks meaning.

AI is not a replacement for human thought – it is an invitation to explore what makes us truly human: our ability to ask '**why?**'

Artificial Intelligence is not a single monolithic entity – it comes in **different forms**, each with its own capabilities, limitations, and implications for the world.

Understanding these forms is like understanding stages of human intelligence, from specialised skills to wisdom that transcends boundaries...

Artificial Narrow Intelligence (ANI)

Artificial Narrow Intelligence is AI designed to perform a **specific task**. It is highly skilled in one domain but lacks general understanding. Think of ANI as a master of one trade, yet completely clueless about everything else.

Human Touch Analogy:

Imagine a brilliant surgeon who can perform heart surgery flawlessly but cannot navigate a car, solve a math problem, or cook a meal. ANI is similar, it excels in one area, but outside that area, it is effectively **'blind.'**

Key Highlights:

1. **Task-specific:** ANI is excellent at narrowly defined problems.

2. **No general understanding:** It cannot apply its knowledge beyond its domain.
3. **Data-driven:** Learns patterns from large datasets.
4. **Examples:**
5. **Voice Assistants:** Siri or Alexa can understand speech commands, but they cannot compose an original poem with philosophical depth.
6. **Recommendation Engines:** Netflix suggests movies based on your history but cannot teach you how to pick stocks.
7. **Self-driving Cars (current versions):** They can navigate roads but cannot autonomously cook dinner or plan a vacation.

ANI is the AI that dominates today's world, highly efficient, practical, and everywhere, yet limited in understanding the broader context of human experience.

Artificial General Intelligence (AGI)

Artificial General Intelligence represents a hypothetical stage of AI where machines would possess human-like cognitive abilities across a broad range of tasks. Unlike Artificial Narrow AI (ANI), which excels only in special domains, AGI would be able to **reason**, **learn from experience**, **adapt to new environments**, and **solve complex problems** without requiring explicit programming. It would demonstrate self-awareness, comprehension, and the capacity to transfer knowledge seamlessly across various domains.

The development of AGI involves advanced **neural architectures**, **self-learning algorithms**, and **cognitive computing models** aimed at replicating human intelligence. However, achieving AGI is an immense challenge due to current technological limitations, restricted computational power, and the profound complexity of human cognition. Scientists and researchers remain divided on whether AGI is even achievable and continue to debate its potential risks, ethical implications, and unintended consequences.

If successfully developed, AGI could transform industries in ways beyond imagination. It could power **AI-driven research assistants** capable of discovering new drugs or diagnosing diseases with unparalleled precision. In creative domains, AGI could compose original music, craft engaging literature, and design visually stunning artwork, vastly expanding the boundaries of human creativity. In finance, it could predict market trends with a deep understanding of economic variables, while in education, AGI-powered tutors could personalise learning experiences on a massive scale.

However, the potential of AGI also introduces significant concerns. Issues like **job displacement**, **decision accountability**, and **control challenges** make governance and regulation crucial before AGI reaches its maturity.

Examples of AGI in Future Use Cases:

1. **Healthcare** – AGI-powered assistants diagnosing rare diseases and recommending personalised treatment plans based on extensive data analysis.
2. **Scientific Research** – AI-driven systems discovering new materials for sustainable energy solutions, accelerating technological progress.
3. **Education** – Intelligent tutoring systems providing customised learning experiences tailored to individual students' strengths and weaknesses.
4. **Space Exploration** – AGI-driven decision-making assisting autonomous spacecraft in planetary exploration and colonisation efforts.
5. **Legal Industry** – AI-powered systems analysing legal cases and drafting contracts with a deep understanding of legal precedents and regulations

Agentic AI

Agentic AI refers to systems capable of **autonomous decision-making**, **strategic goal-setting**, and **independent problem-solving**. Unlike conventional AI, which follows predefined rules and models, agentic AI interacts dynamically with its environment, assesses situations, and takes proactive actions to achieve specific objectives. This makes it far more **adaptive** and **self-reliant** compared to traditional AI systems.

Agentic AI frequently leverages **reinforcement learning**, **multi-agent systems**, and **decision-theoretic planning**. These approaches make it highly useful in fields like **robotics**, **autonomous vehicles**, **financial trading**, and **cybersecurity**. For example, **self-driving cars** powered by agentic AI can analyse traffic, predict driver behaviours, and make split-second decisions to prevent accidents, while in cybersecurity, it autonomously detects and counter cyber threats in real-time without requiring human input.

While offering tremendous potential, agentic AI also raises pressing ethical and accountability concerns. In financial markets, AI systems executing high-speed trades could unintentionally destabilize economies. In military applications, autonomous drones making real time combat decisions raise complex moral dilemmas. Ensuring agentic AI aligns with human interests and ethical principles remains an ongoing challenge.

Examples of Agentic AI in Future Use Cases:

1. **Autonomous Vehicles** – Self-driving trucks managing logistics and supply chains through real-time decision-making.
2. **Cybersecurity** – AI-driven threat detection systems autonomously neutralizing cyberattacks without human oversight.
3. **Smart Cities** – AI-powered traffic management optimising routes, reducing congestion, and lowering emissions.
4. **Autonomous Finance** – AI-powered trading bots executing investment strategies with advanced, real-time market analysis.

5. **Disaster Response** – AI-driven drones and robots coordinating emergency relief efforts during natural disasters.

Artificial Super Intelligence (ASI)

Artificial Super Intelligence represents a theoretical future stage where machines surpass human intelligence in every dimension, including **cognitive reasoning**, **creativity**, and **emotional understanding**. ASI would outperform humans in problem-solving, decision-making, and self-improvement while also possessing capabilities far beyond human comprehension.

The development of ASI has the potential to drive unprecedented scientific breakthroughs and accelerate technological innovation. For example, ASI could help address global challenges like **climate change** by simulating complex environmental modelling and developing effective solutions. In healthcare, ASI could create cures for incurable diseases and design hyper-personalised treatment plans tailored to each individual's genetic makeup. In engineering, it could conceptualise and build advanced materials and structures beyond human capability, revolutionising industries worldwide.

However, ASI also poses profound existential risks. A superintelligent system with **self-improving capabilities** could evolve at an uncontrollable pace, making decisions that prioritise efficiency over human values. This raises critical debates about **AI alignment**, **governance**, and **safety protocols** to ensure that ASI, when achieved, benefits humanity rather than threatens it.

Examples of ASI in Future Use Cases:

1. **Global Problem-Solving** – ASI predicting and mitigating natural disasters through advanced climate modelling and intervention strategies.
2. **Advanced Scientific Discoveries** – SuperIntelligent AI formulating theories beyond current human comprehension, pushing the frontiers of physics and space exploration.
3. **Human-Machine Symbiosis** – AI integrating with human cognition to enhance mental abilities and extend human lifespan.
4. **Automated Governance** – AI-driven policy-making optimising government decisions, resource allocation, and economic growth.

5. **Interstellar Colonisation** – ASI planning and executing large-scale space colonisation to ensure humanity's survival beyond Earth.

Chapter 02

AI and its Future Technology

AI and Its Future Technology

Excerpt from 'AI - The Code of WHY?'

Artificial Intelligence is no longer a futuristic concept; it has become the engine transforming the way we live, work, and think. In *AI - The Code of WHY?* we explore not just the mechanics of AI, but the deeper reasons why it matters: how it learns, why it makes decisions, and how it shapes the future of human society.

A Legacy of Visionaries

The journey of AI began with the visionaries who dared to imagine machines that could think. **John McCarthy**, often called the father of AI, defined it in 1955 as 'the science and engineering of making intelligent machines.' McCarthy's goal was not just computation; it was the creation of systems capable of reasoning, learning, and adapting.

Following McCarthy, pioneers like **Marvin Minsky**, **Alan Turing**, and **Geoffrey Hinton** laid the foundations for neural networks, machine learning, and deep learning, enabling today's AI to recognise speech, translate languages, drive cars autonomously, and even generate creative content. In ***'AI - The Code of WHY?'***, we emphasise understanding these foundations to appreciate the 'why' behind AI's actions.

AI Today: Practical Intelligence

Modern AI is deeply embedded in our daily lives and business processes. Key applications include:

1. **Machine Learning (ML)**: Algorithms that learn from data and improve autonomously. For instance, Netflix uses ML to personalise recommendations, keeping viewers engaged.
2. **Natural Language Processing (NLP)**: Machines can now understand and interact in human language. ChatGPT, a prime example, shows how AI can communicate naturally and assist in problem-solving.
3. **Computer Vision**: AI interprets visual data for tasks like autonomous driving or quality inspection in manufacturing.

4. **Generative AI**: AI now creates text, images, music, and even software code, enabling innovation in arts, research, and business.

The Future of AI Technology

The future of AI is defined by **intelligence that collaborates with humans**. Emerging trends include:

1. **Explainable AI (XAI)**: Understanding the 'why' behind AI decisions, crucial for healthcare, finance, and governance.
2. **AI + Quantum Computing**: Solving previously intractable problems like climate modelling, material science, or genome sequencing.
3. **Autonomous Systems**: Self-driving vehicles, intelligent drones, and factories operating independently yet safely.
4. **AI for Global Challenges**: Predicting natural disasters, accelerating medical discoveries, and optimising resource usage for sustainability.

Benefits of AI in Real Life

In '***AI - The Code of WHY?***' we highlight how AI benefits humans and businesses:

- **Efficiency & Productivity**: Automating repetitive tasks to focus human creativity where it matters. For example, AI-driven automation in banking reduces manual processing by 70%.
- **Personalised Experiences**: Amazon's AI-driven recommendations enhance customer engagement and increase sales.
- **Innovation Acceleration**: AI accelerates research in drug discovery, space exploration, and software development.
- **Informed Decisions**: Predictive analytics enables smarter decisions, minimising risk while maximising outcomes.

Human-Centric AI: Collaboration over Replacement

AI's greatest potential emerges when it **augments human intelligence** rather than replaces it. As Andrew Ng states, 'AI is the new electricity.' In the context of this book, we see AI as a **partner that amplifies human reasoning**, creativity, and insight.

The challenge for the next generation of AI is ensuring its ethical and responsible use, meaning it must remain transparent, fair, and aligned with human values. In '***AI - The Code of WHY?***' we explore not just how AI works, but **why it works**, helping readers understand its impact, limitations, and promise.

Conclusion

AI is more than technology; it is a collaborator, a guide, and a tool for human progress. From McCarthy's vision to modern generative AI, the journey of intelligence is accelerating. In ***'AI - The Code of WHY?',*** we aim to decode AI's mysteries, exploring its principles, potential, and the profound 'why' behind every action it takes. The future will be defined not just by what AI can do, but by **how humans choose to harness it responsibly and creatively**.

AI in Everyday Life: How it's Already Shaping Our Future?

Excerpt from 'AI- The Code of WHY?'

Artificial Intelligence may seem like a futuristic concept, but in reality, it is already deeply woven into the fabric of our daily lives. In '***AI - The Code of WHY?'*** we aim to go beyond the surface of 'how' AI works and explore the '***why***' behind its decisions, interactions, and transformative impact.

Why AI in Communication and Productivity?

Whether we realise it or not, AI helps us communicate, organise, and work more efficiently:

- **Virtual Assistants** like Siri, Alexa, and Google Assistant use AI to understand our requests, schedule appointments, and even predict our needs. The 'why' behind these tools is to **reduce**

cognitive load, letting humans focus on creativity and decision-making.

- **Email Filtering & Smart Replies** rely on Natural Language Processing (NLP) to sort spam and suggest quick responses. By learning from our habits, AI reduces repetitive effort, saving **hours of work each week**.

Why AI in Entertainment and Personalisation?

AI shapes our media and entertainment in subtle yet profound ways:

1. **Streaming Recommendations**: Netflix and Spotify use machine learning to analyse our preferences and suggest content we are likely to enjoy. By understanding 'why' these systems make recommendations, we see AI as a **personalised guide**, curating experiences tailored to our tastes.
2. **Gaming**: Modern video games use AI to create dynamic, responsive worlds. Characters learn from

players' actions, providing experiences that feel organic and immersive.

Why AI in Everyday Services?

AI's reach extends into many services we interact with daily, often invisibly:

1. **Navigation & Transportation**: Google Maps and ride-sharing apps like Uber use AI to optimise routes, predict traffic, and reduce travel time. The underlying **'why'** is **efficiency and better decision-making** for every journey.
2. **Banking & Fraud Detection**: AI monitors transactions in real-time to detect unusual patterns, preventing fraud and protecting users. Here, AI acts as a **guardian**, learning continuously from emerging threats.

Why AI in Health and Well-Being?

Healthcare is one of the most profound areas where AI demonstrates its value:

1. **Predictive Diagnostics**: AI analyses medical images and patient data to detect early signs of diseases like cancer or diabetic retinopathy. Understanding the **'why'** behind AI's predictions allows doctors to make **faster, more accurate decisions**, potentially saving lives.
2. **Virtual Health Assistants**: AI-powered chatbots provide guidance, monitor patient conditions, and support mental health initiatives. These systems amplify human care, making healthcare more accessible and personalised.

Why AI as a Human Collaborator?

In ***'AI – The Code of WHY?'***, one of our core messages is that AI is **not a replacement for humans**, but a partner that augments our capabilities. From managing mundane tasks to providing insights and predictions, AI frees humans to focus on creativity, empathy, and critical thinking – qualities machines cannot replicate.

Conclusion

Every day, AI touches lives in ways that often go unnoticed, improving efficiency, personalisation, and safety. By exploring the **why behind AI** in everyday applications**, *'AI – The Code of WHY?',*** helps readers understand both the **mechanics and the meaning** of AI. This understanding empowers us to use AI responsibly, creatively, and ethically, shaping a future where technology amplifies human potential rather than diminishes it.

AI in Business and Industry: Why We Need It and How It Transforms the World?

Excerpt from 'AI – The Code of WHY?'

In today's rapidly evolving business landscape, the question is no longer **'if'** AI should be adopted, but **'why not'**. Businesses that embrace AI are not just optimising operations; they are reshaping entire industries, creating new revenue streams, and unlocking opportunities that were previously unimaginable. In ***'AI – The Code of WHY?',*** we explore why AI is essential in business and industry, and how it can transform organisations from being reactive to truly predictive and proactive.

Why Businesses Need AI?

1. **The Complexity of Modern Business**

   Global business operations are increasingly complex, involving vast amounts of data, supply chain dependencies, and rapidly changing customer expectations. Humans alone cannot process and interpret this information efficiently. AI provides the ability to **analyse massive datasets in real -time**, uncover hidden patterns, and make decisions that drive competitive advantage.

   For example, retailers like Amazon use AI to predict customer demand, optimise inventory, and manage logistics, ensuring that products are available where and when customers want them. Understanding the 'why' behind this application reveals a deeper principle: AI allows businesses to **operate with foresight rather than hindsight**, making them agile and resilient.

2. **Personalisation at Scale**

   Customers today expect experiences tailored to their preferences. Traditional methods of segmentation and targeting cannot keep up with this expectation. AI enables hyper-personalisation by analysing individual behaviour and predicting needs.

   Example: Spotify and Netflix use AI-driven recommendation engines to create experiences unique to each user.

i. **Business Impact:** Personalised experiences drive **higher engagement, customer loyalty, and revenue**. AI is no longer a luxury; it is a **necessity** for companies that want to retain and grow their customer base in competitive markets.

3. **Operational Efficiency and Cost Reduction**

   Businesses operate in a world of limited resources

and increasing cost pressures. AI can automate repetitive, labour-intensive tasks, reducing errors and freeing employees to focus on strategic, value-added activities.

Example: In banking, AI-powered Robotic Process Automation (RPA) processes thousands of loan applications daily, ensuring accuracy and speeding up approvals.

a) **Business Impact:** Organisations save millions annually while improving service quality and compliance.

4. **Data-Driven Decision Making**

   Decision-making in business often suffers from incomplete information, bias, or slow analysis. AI turns raw data into actionable insights, providing leaders with predictive analytics, risk assessment, and scenario modelling.

   i. **Example:** Airlines use AI to forecast ticket demand, optimise pricing, and plan fleet usage.

5. **Business Impact:** Enhanced decision-making **reduces risk, maximises profits, and improves operational efficiency**.

How AI Transforms Industries?

1. **Manufacturing**

   AI in manufacturing; sometimes called 'Industry 4.0,' optimises production, reduces waste, and predicts maintenance needs:

i. **Predictive Maintenance:** Sensors combined with AI algorithms detect potential equipment failures before they occur.

ii. **Quality Control:** Computer vision inspects products for defects, ensuring higher quality and reducing returns.

iii. **Supply Chain Optimisation:** AI predicts demand fluctuations, optimising inventory and reducing costs.

2. **Healthcare**

   AI is revolutionising healthcare by improving

diagnostics, treatment planning, and operational efficiency:

i. **Predictive Diagnostics:** AI analyses medical images and patient data to identify diseases early.
ii. **Operational Efficiency:** Hospitals use AI to optimise staff allocation, patient flow, and resource management.
iii. **Research & Drug Discovery:** AI accelerates the identification of potential compounds, significantly reducing the time required for drug development.

3. **Finance**

The financial sector relies heavily on AI to detect fraud, optimise investment strategies, and enhance customer service:

i. **Fraud Detection:** Machine learning identifies unusual transaction patterns in real-time.
ii. **Customer Insights:** AI analyses spending behaviour to suggest relevant financial products.
iii. **Algorithmic Trading:** AI predicts market trends, enabling faster, more informed trading decisions.

4. **Retail and E-Commerce**

   AI is at the heart of retail innovation:

i. **Inventory Management:** AI predicts what products will be in demand and where, reducing overstock or stockouts.
ii. **Personalised Marketing:** AI delivers targeted promotions based on customer behaviour.
iii. **Customer Service:** Chatbots powered by AI resolve queries instantly, enhancing satisfaction.

5. **Energy and Utilities**

   AI enables smarter energy management and operational efficiency:

i. **Smart Grids:** AI predicts energy demand and adjusts distribution in real-time.
ii. **Predictive Maintenance:** AI monitors equipment to prevent downtime in power plants.
iii. **Energy Optimisation:** AI models optimise energy usage in large buildings or industrial plants, reducing costs and environmental impact.

The Benefits of AI in Business: More than Just Numbers

While the financial impact of AI is clear, its benefits go far beyond cost savings:

1. **Innovation Enablement:** AI accelerates the development of new products, services, and business models.
2. **Competitive Advantage:** Companies using AI strategically outperform peers, often capturing greater market share.
3. **Human Empowerment:** By handling repetitive tasks, AI allows employees to focus on creativity, problem-solving, and strategy.
4. **Sustainability:** AI helps organisations reduce waste, optimise resources, and operate more sustainably.

AI as a Strategic Imperative?

In ***'AI – The Code of WHY?'***, we emphasise that adopting AI is no longer optional, it is a strategic imperative. Businesses that ignore AI risk falling behind, while those that embrace it can:

i. Respond to market changes faster
ii. Deliver superior customer experiences
iii. Optimise operations and resources
iv. Innovate continuously and responsibly

As **Andrew Ng** famously said, 'AI is the new electricity.' Just as electricity transformed every industry a century ago, AI is now transforming business. Companies that understand **why** AI matters, and apply it thoughtfully, will define the next era of innovation.

Conclusion

AI is not just a tool – it is a **strategic partner** for modern businesses. From manufacturing floors to financial markets, from healthcare to retail, AI is enabling smarter decisions, faster operations, and personalised experiences. In ***'AI – The Code of WHY?'***, we explore how businesses can harness AI responsibly, creatively, and ethically, ensuring it complements human intelligence rather than replacing it.

The future of industry belongs to organisations that embrace AI not only to improve efficiency, but to **reimagine the very way they create value**. Understanding the ***'why'*** behind AI is the first step towards building a business that is not just profitable, but resilient, innovative, and future-ready.

AI in Decision Making: How Machines Can Help Humans Think Smarter?

Excerpt from 'AI – The Code of WHY?'

In ***'AI – The Code of WHY?'***, one of the central themes is understanding **why AI matters in our lives and work**. Decision-making is at the heart of almost every human activity, whether it's running a business, managing a city, or making personal choices. Today, AI is not replacing human judgement; it is **augmenting it**, helping us make smarter, faster, and more informed decisions.

Why Humans Need AI in Decision Making?

1. **Complexity Beyond Human Capacity**
   Modern environments, such as business, healthcare, finance, and more generate vast amounts of data every second. Humans cannot process this volume and complexity alone, so AI analyses enormous datasets, uncovers hidden patterns, and provides insights that would take humans years to discover.

   Example: Financial institutions use AI to detect anomalies in millions of transactions, identifying potential fraud in real time. The 'why' is clear: **AI empowers humans to act before a problem escalates**, minimising risk.

2. **Bias Reduction and Objectivity**
   Human decisions are often influenced by emotions, cognitive biases, or incomplete information. AI, when designed responsibly, provides objective recommendations based on data and patterns.

Example: In recruitment, AI tools analyse candidate profiles for skills and experience, reducing unconscious bias in initial screening. Here, AI helps humans make **fairer and more data-driven decisions**.

3. **Predictive Power**

   AI can predict outcomes based on historical and real-time data, enabling proactive decisions rather than reactive ones.

   Example: Retailers like Walmart use AI to forecast demand for products, ensuring inventory matches customer needs. Predictive AI allows businesses to **anticipate rather than react**, saving costs and improving customer satisfaction.

How AI Supports Decision Making?

1. **Data-Driven Insights**

   AI can convert raw data into actionable intelligence. Tools like predictive analytics, machine learning models, and dashboards help decision-makers **see the story behind the numbers**.

Example: Healthcare providers use AI to analyse patient records and predict hospital readmission risks, allowing interventions that improve patient outcomes.

2. **Scenario Simulation and Optimisation**
   AI enables businesses to simulate multiple scenarios, weighing different outcomes before committing to a decision.

   Example: Airlines use AI to model flight schedules under different weather conditions, optimising routes and minimising delays.

3. **Real-Time Decision Support**
   In fast-moving industries, decisions must be made quickly. AI systems can provide real-time recommendations and alerts.

   Example: Stock trading platforms use AI to instantly analyse market movements and provide recommendations to traders with a **speed and precision** beyond human capability.

4. **Collaborative Decision Making**

   AI acts as a partner, not a replacement. It can suggest options, highlight risks, and even point out overlooked opportunities. Humans retain ultimate judgement, while AI enhances the quality and speed of decisions.

   Example: In supply chain management, AI identifies potential disruptions and recommends alternative routes. Managers still decide, but with **better information and reduced uncertainty**.

Benefits of AI-Augmented Decision Making

1. **Increased Accuracy:** AI reduces errors caused by human fatigue or oversight.
2. **Time Efficiency:** Automates data analysis, freeing humans to focus on strategy.
3. **Risk Mitigation:** Predicts potential issues and provides solutions proactively.

4. **Innovation Enablement:** By handling routine analysis, AI allows humans to explore creative and high-value decisions.

Expert Insights: The Wisdom Behind AI Decisions

The father of AI, John McCarthy, emphasised that machines should **augment human intelligence**, not replace it. Similarly, AI thought leaders like Andrew Ng and Geoffrey Hinton advocate using AI to **extend our reasoning abilities**, enabling humans to make better decisions faster.

1. **Andrew Ng:** 'AI is about making people more productive, not obsolete.'
2. **Geoffrey Hinton:** 'AI is a tool for amplifying human intelligence, not a substitute for it.'

In ***'AI – The Code of WHY?'*** we focus on decoding these principles, showing readers how understanding **why AI**

makes recommendations allows humans to trust, interpret, and act on AI insights responsibly.

Conclusion

AI is not just a computational engine; it is a **decision partner**. In complex, data-rich environments, humans need AI to **see patterns, predict outcomes, and optimise choices**. From healthcare to finance, logistics to customer service, AI empowers smarter decisions that improve efficiency, reduce risk, and create opportunities for innovation.

In ***'AI – The Code of WHY?',*** understanding the **'why'** behind AI's decisions is critical. Only by grasping its reasoning can humans collaborate effectively with machines, unlocking the true potential of AI as an **intelligent assistant, guide, and enabler**.

The next chapters of this book continue exploring how AI interacts with human creativity, problem-solving, and ethical considerations, ensuring we harness its power **responsibly and meaningfully**.

AI in Creativity and Innovation: Why It Matters?

Excerpt from 'AI – The Code of WHY?'

When we think of Artificial Intelligence, many imagine it as a tool for automation, efficiency, or analytics. But **in *'AI – The Code of WHY?'*,** we explore a deeper truth: AI is also a catalyst for **creativity and innovation**. The question is not just ***what AI can do***, but **why, AI is essential for human innovation in the modern world**.

Why AI is Important for Creativity?

1. **Expanding Human Imagination**
   Human creativity has always been constrained by time, resources, and knowledge. AI expands these boundaries by offering insights, suggestions, and alternatives that humans might never consider on their own.

   Example: In design and architecture, generative AI can create hundreds of variations of a product or building layout in minutes. Architects can then select and refine the most promising options.

The Why: AI acts as a **creative partner**, extending the scope of human imagination and making innovation faster and more diverse.

2. **Enhancing Problem-Solving**

   Innovation often begins with solving a complex problem. AI can analyse large datasets, identify patterns, and simulate outcomes to propose novel solutions.

   Example: Pharmaceutical companies use AI to explore millions of molecular combinations, speeding up the discovery of new drugs.

   The Why: AI accelerates experimentation, helping humans **innovate solutions that were previously impossible due to scale, scope, or complexity**.

3. **Amplifying Human Creativity**

   AI does not replace creativity, it amplifies it. By handling repetitive or data-intensive tasks, AI frees humans to focus on high-level thinking and ideation.

Example: In music and art, AI tools like OpenAI's MuseNet or DALL·E generate compositions and visuals that inspire artists to create new works.

The Why: AI transforms creativity from a solitary process into a collaborative journey between human insight and machine intelligence.

Why Businesses and Industries Need AI-Driven Innovation?

1. **Staying Competitive in a Rapidly Changing World**
   Markets today evolve faster than ever. Companies that fail to innovate quickly risk obsolescence. AI provides the speed, insight, and predictive power needed to **anticipate trends, experiment safely, and pivot rapidly**.

Example: Retailers use AI to analyse consumer behaviour and launch personalised campaigns or products before competitors.

The Why: AI ensures that businesses are not just reacting to change but are **leading it with data-driven creativity**.

2. **Reducing Risk in Innovation**

   Innovation involves experimentation, which inherently carries risk. AI can simulate outcomes, optimise designs, and predict results, reducing failure and maximising success.

   Example: Automotive companies use AI-driven simulations to test thousands of crash scenarios virtually before physical prototypes are built.

   The Why: AI enables **smarter, safer experimentation**, allowing humans to innovate confidently and efficiently.

3. **Creating New Possibilities**

   AI opens doors to entirely new fields and business

models, creating opportunities that would be impossible to imagine without it.

Example: Generative AI has enabled companies to create virtual fashion, AI-generated content, and entirely new digital products.

- **The Why:** AI is a tool for **expanding human potential**, allowing creativity to scale beyond traditional limits.

Expert Insights: Why AI is Essential for Innovation?

The visionaries of AI have always emphasised its potential to **augment human intelligence, not replace it**:

- **John McCarthy:** AI should enable humans to solve problems that are too large or complex to handle alone.
- **Geoffrey Hinton:** AI can 'unlock new ways of thinking' and help humans explore ideas faster and more creatively.

- **Andrew Ng:** AI is the tool that amplifies human talent, transforming creativity and innovation into measurable outcomes.

In ***'AI- The Code of WHY?'***, understanding **why AI works the way it does** allows innovators to trust and collaborate with it effectively. The ***'why'*** ensures that AI is used responsibly and ethically while still pushing, the boundaries of what is possible.

Conclusion

Why We Need AI for the Future of Innovation

AI is not just a computational tool – it is a **creative partner, an idea generator, and a risk reducer**. It allows humans to explore more possibilities, solve complex problems faster, and bring ideas to life in ways that were unimaginable a decade ago.

In ***'AI – The Code of WHY?',*** the core message is clear: AI matters because it enables humans to **think bigger, act smarter, and create with confidence**. It transforms innovation from a slow, trial-and-error process into a **collaborative journey between human insight and machine intelligence**.

The future of creativity belongs to those who understand **why AI works, why it is essential, and how to harness it responsibly**. Only then can we unlock the full potential of human imagination, amplified by intelligent machines.

AI in Creativity and Innovation: Why It is Critical for the Future?

Excerpt from 'AI – The Code of WHY?'

Creativity and innovation are the lifeblood of human progress. Throughout history, every leap from the printing press to the internet has been driven by humans imagining the yet-to-exist. But in today's rapidly evolving world, imagination alone is no longer enough. The problems we face are too complex, the pace of change too fast, and the scale of possibilities too vast. This is precisely **why AI is essential**.

In ***'AI – The Code of WHY?',*** we explore not just how AI functions, but also why it is an indispensable partner in modern creativity and innovation. AI is not here to replace human ingenuity, it is here to **amplify it, accelerate it, and unlock possibilities humans could never achieve alone**.

Why AI is a Game-Changer in Creativity?

1. **Expanding the Horizon of Human Imagination**
   Humans naturally think linearly, constrained by prior knowledge, experience, and cognitive limits. AI, however, can process **millions of variables and generate possibilities in seconds**.

   Example: In product design, generative AI can produce hundreds of prototypes for a single concept, each with subtle variations. Designers can then select and refine the most promising ideas, exponentially increasing the **breadth and quality of creative options**.

The Why: AI **enables humans to imagine beyond their natural limits**, turning possibilities into actionable designs, solutions, or concepts.

2. **Accelerating Problem-Solving**

   Innovation often starts with identifying problems and testing solutions. Traditionally, experimentation is slow, costly, and limited in scale. AI changes this:

   Example: In pharmaceuticals, AI models can simulate thousands of chemical combinations to identify promising drug candidates, a process that would take humans years to perform manually.

   The Why: AI **reduces trial-and-error cycles**, allowing humans to focus on the most impactful solutions and accelerating breakthroughs.

3. **Amplifying Human Creativity**

   AI handles data-intensive, repetitive, or computationally heavy tasks, freeing humans to focus on strategy, design, and high-level ideation.

Example: Musicians, artists, and writers use AI to generate novel melodies, visual concepts, or storylines, which they then adapt and enhance. The AI acts as a **collaborative assistant**, not a replacement.

The Why: By managing the heavy lifting, AI **amplifies human creativity**, transforming raw imagination into refined, executable innovation.

Why Businesses and Industries Cannot Ignore AI-Driven Innovation?

1. **Staying Competitive in a Rapidly Changing World**
   Markets and industries evolve faster than ever. Companies that fail to innovate quickly risk obsolescence while AI equips organisations to **anticipate trends, identify opportunities, and act decisively**.

   Example: Retailers like Amazon and Alibaba use AI to monitor global consumer behaviour, predict demand, and develop products ahead of competitors.

The Why: AI transforms businesses from reactive entities into proactive innovators, **future-proofing operations and strategies**.

2. **Reducing Risk in Innovation**

   Experimentation is inherently risky. AI reduces uncertainty by modelling scenarios, simulating outcomes, and providing data-driven recommendations.

   Example: Automotive companies simulate thousands of crash-test scenarios using AI, identifying the safest designs before producing physical prototypes.

   The Why: AI **minimises risk while maximising** learning, enabling safer and more confident innovation.

3. **Enabling Completely New Possibilities**

   AI does not just optimise existing ideas it opens

doors to entirely new concepts, business models, and industries.

Example: Generative AI has created virtual fashion lines, AI-generated films, and personalised digital experiences, launching industries that were unimaginable a decade ago.

The Why: AI is a **catalyst for entirely new forms of human expression and enterprise**, extending creativity beyond traditional boundaries.

Expert Perspectives on Why AI Matters in Innovation?

1. **John McCarthy (Father of AI):** Machines should help humans solve problems too large or complex to tackle alone.
2. **Geoffrey Hinton:** AI can unlock new ways of thinking, enhancing human problem-solving and creative reasoning.

3. **Andrew Ng:** AI is the tool that amplifies human potential, transforming imagination into tangible innovation.

In ***'AI – The Code of WHY?',*** understanding **why AI operates the way it does** allows humans to trust it, collaborate with it, and use it responsibly. The ***'why'*** is not technical – it is **strategic, ethical, and human-centered**.

The Benefits of AI in Creativity and Innovation

- **Exponential Idea Generation:** AI generates possibilities humans may never conceive.
- **Faster Experimentation:** AI reduces the time between concept and execution.
- **Smarter Problem-Solving:** AI provides insights that guide better decisions.
- **Risk Mitigation:** AI simulates outcomes, allowing safer experimentation.
- **Scalable Innovation:** AI helps small teams create solutions that can impact millions.

Conclusion

Why AI is Essential for the Future of Innovation

AI is not just a tool for efficiency – it is a **partner for human imagination, a collaborator in problem-solving, and a force multiplier for innovation**. In ***'AI – The Code of WHY?'***, we stress that AI matters because it **enables humans to dream bigger, act smarter, and create with confidence**.

The future of creativity and innovation belongs to those who understand **why AI works, why it is necessary, and how to harness it responsibly**. Only by decoding the **'why'** can humans collaborate effectively with machines, transforming ideas into solutions, and making the impossible possible.

AI is not just a technology – it is a **bridge between human potential and limitless possibility**. Understanding its why is the first step toward mastering its power.

AI and Ethics: Why Understanding the Why is Critical?

Excerpt from 'AI- The Code of WHY?'

Artificial Intelligence is transforming every aspect of our lives, from how we work to how we communicate, learn, and create. But as AI becomes more powerful, the question is no longer just *can it do something*, but **should it do it?** In ***'AI- The Code of WHY?'***, understanding **why AI matters** goes hand-in-hand with understanding **why AI must be used responsibly**. Ethics is not a constraint – it is the guiding principle that ensures AI fulfils its potential in a way that aligns with human values.

Why Ethics is Essential in AI

1. **AI Influences Human Lives at Scale**
   AI decisions increasingly affect employment, healthcare, finance, and social interactions. Without ethical frameworks, a seemingly neutral algorithm can unintentionally **disadvantage certain groups or amplify biases**.

Example: Credit scoring algorithms may unfairly deny loans to certain demographics if trained on biased historical data.

The Why: Ethics ensures that AI systems are **fair, inclusive, and accountable**, protecting human rights and dignity.

2. **Complexity and Lack of Transparency**

   AI models, especially deep learning systems, are often 'black boxes,' making it difficult to understand their reasoning. Without ethical guidance, humans may **blindly trust decisions without questioning the underlying logic**.

   Example: An AI used in criminal justice to predict recidivism might influence sentencing, yet its decision-making process could be opaque.

   The Why: Ethics emphasises **explainability**, so humans can understand, validate, and trust AI decisions.

3. **Responsibility and Accountability**

   AI is not autonomous in the moral sense, humans design, deploy, and maintain these systems. Understanding **why we build AI the way we do** is critical to assigning responsibility and ensuring accountability.

   Example: Autonomous vehicles may face situations where harm is unavoidable. Ethical design principles determine how the vehicle prioritises outcomes.

   The Why: Ethics ensures that humans remain **accountable for AI actions**, preventing misuse or negligence.

Why Understanding the Why Matters in AI Ethics

1. **Aligning AI with Human Values**

   AI should reflect society's values: fairness, transparency, privacy, and inclusivity. When we ask **why AI makes decisions**, we can evaluate whether those decisions align with our ethical expectations.

Example: Healthcare AI predicting patient treatment plans must balance accuracy with patient safety and consent.

The Why: By focusing on the 'why,' developers ensure AI **enhances well-being rather than causing harm**.

2. **Preventing Bias and Discrimination**
   AI learns from data, but if the data reflects societal biases, AI can perpetuate or amplify them. Understanding **why the AI reaches certain conclusions** allows humans to detect bias and correct it.

   Example: Facial recognition systems have historically underperformed on darker skin tones. By analysing the ***'why'*** behind errors, engineers can retrain models with more inclusive datasets.

   The Why: Ethics ensures AI is **equitable and trustworthy**, not just technically efficient.

3. **Building Trust in AI Systems**

   AI adoption depends on trust. Users need to understand why AI makes recommendations or predictions, and developers must ensure decisions are **transparent and accountable**.

   Example: In financial advising, AI tools explain investment suggestions based on historical trends, risk appetite, and portfolio goals.

   The Why: Clear reasoning builds **user confidence**, ensuring AI is accepted as a reliable collaborator rather than a mysterious oracle.

The Benefits of Ethical AI

1. **Human-Centric Innovation:** Ethical AI ensures innovation **serves people**, not just efficiency or profit.
2. **Sustainable Impact:** AI decisions that respect societal values create long-term benefits for organisations and communities.
3. **Resilience Against Risk:** Ethical oversight minimises legal, reputational, and operational risks.

4. **Inclusive Growth:** AI can democratise opportunities, ensuring benefits reach a broader population.

Expert Insights: Why Ethics is Integral to AI

1. **John McCarthy** envisioned AI as a tool to extend human intelligence, not replace moral judgement.
2. **Stuart Russell**, AI thought leader, emphasises that AI systems must be designed to **align with human values**, preventing unintended consequences.
3. **Timnit Gebru**, AI ethics researcher, highlights that understanding **why AI decisions happen** is essential for fairness, accountability, and social responsibility.

In ***'AI – The Code of WHY?'***, the emphasis is clear: **understanding the why behind AI decisions is not optional, it is critical**. Without this understanding, AI becomes a tool that acts blindly, rather than a partner that augments human potential responsibly.

Conclusion

Why AI Ethics Defines the Future

AI has immense power to transform industries, solve complex problems, and augment human creativity. But this power comes with responsibility. The ***'why'*** behind AI the reasoning, the purpose, the decision-making process must be understood, guided, and aligned with ethical principles.

In ***'AI – The Code of WHY?'***, ethics is presented not as a limitation, but as the **foundation for meaningful innovation**. By asking **why AI acts, why it is trusted, and why it matters**, humans can harness AI safely, creatively, and responsibly. This ensures that AI serves humanity, amplifies our potential, and contributes positively to society.

Ethics is the compass, and understanding the ***'why'*** is the map together, they guide AI toward a future that is **innovative, inclusive, and human-centered**.

AI and Human Potential: Why We Need AI to Unlock Our Best Capabilities?

Excerpt from ***'AI–The Code of WHY?'***

Artificial Intelligence is often portrayed as a replacement for human work, a system that will take over tasks and render human effort obsolete. In ***'AI- The Code of WHY?'***, we challenge this perception. The true purpose of AI is not to replace humans, but to **unlock the best of human potential**. The question we must ask is not what AI can do alone, but why AI is essential for helping humans achieve more, think deeper, and create greater value in the world.

Why AI Matters for Human Potential

1. **Amplifying Cognitive Abilities**
   Humans have immense creativity and problem-solving ability, but our cognitive resources are limited. AI extends our capacity by analysing vast

datasets, detecting patterns, and offering insights that would take humans years to uncover.

Example: In scientific research, AI can process millions of studies and experiments to identify novel correlations, guiding researchers to breakthroughs faster.

The Why: AI acts as a **cognitive partner**, allowing humans to focus on interpretation, creativity, and strategic thinking rather than tedious analysis.

2. **Enhancing Decision-Making**

   Even the most experienced humans can struggle with complex decisions, especially when faced with large amounts of data or uncertainty. AI provides predictive insights, scenario analysis, and optimisation suggestions to support better decision-making.

   Example: Hospitals use AI to prioritise patients based on real-time risk predictions, helping doctors make informed choices under pressure.

The Why: AI enables humans to **decide smarter, faster, and with greater confidence**, turning complexity into actionable understanding.

3. **Enabling Creativity and Innovation**

   Innovation requires exploring new ideas and possibilities, often at scales that exceed human capacity. AI can generate options, test hypotheses, and simulate outcomes, sparking creativity in ways humans alone cannot.

   Example: In architecture, AI can propose hundreds of design variations for a single building concept, allowing architects to explore unconventional approaches.

   The Why: AI is a **creative amplifier**, providing humans with the freedom to experiment, refine, and innovate beyond traditional limits.

How AI Unlocks Potential in Work and Life

1. **Reducing Repetition and Cognitive Load**

   Routine tasks occupy significant mental bandwidth.

AI automates these processes, freeing humans to focus on high-value, meaningful work.

Example: In finance, AI automates data reconciliation and reporting, allowing analysts to concentrate on strategy and investment insights.

The Why: By handling repetitive work, AI **frees humans to think, create, and innovate**, maximising our intellectual potential.

2. **Supporting Learning and Growth**

   AI systems can personalise learning experiences, adapting to individual strengths and weaknesses. This enables continuous growth and development at an unprecedented scale.

   Example: AI-driven educational platforms customise learning paths for students, recommending resources based on progress and comprehension.

The Why: AI acts as a **mentor and guide**, helping humans reach their fullest potential through personalised, actionable insights.

3. **Bridging Knowledge Gaps**

   In a world of exponential knowledge growth, no individual can master all information. AI consolidates, synthesises, and presents insights, bridging gaps in understanding.

   Example: AI-assisted legal research tools summarise thousands of case laws, highlighting relevant precedents for lawyers.

   The Why: AI is a **knowledge accelerator**, allowing humans to make connections and decisions that would be otherwise impossible.

Expert Perspectives on AI and Human Potential

1. **John McCarthy** emphasised that AI should extend human intelligence rather than replace it.

2. **Andrew Ng** calls AI the new electricity, amplifying human productivity and capability across every domain.
3. **Geoffrey Hinton** believes AI can unlock new ways of thinking, enabling humans to solve problems previously considered unsolvable.

In ***'AI – The Code of WHY?'***, we stress that understanding **why AI exists and how it augments human potential** is crucial. Only by knowing the why can humans harness AI responsibly, creatively, and effectively.

Conclusion

Why We Need AI to Reach Our Best Potential?

AI is more than a tool for automation or efficiency. It is a **partner for human growth, creativity, and achievement**. By handling complex calculations, repetitive tasks, and data-heavy analysis, AI allows humans to focus on insight, judgement, and imagination.

The real power of AI lies in its ability to **amplify what humans are naturally good at** while supplementing areas where we are limited. In *AI – The Code of WHY?* the key message is clear: understanding the why behind AI enables humans to collaborate with it responsibly, ethically, and creatively, unlocking potential that was previously unreachable.

AI is not replacing us. It is helping us become the best versions of ourselves. It is **the partner we need to think bigger, act smarter, and create the future we imagine**.

Why Artificial General Intelligence (AGI)?

Artificial General Intelligence, often referred to as AGI, represents machines that possess the capability to perform any intellectual task that humans can accomplish. These systems are designed with human-like cognitive abilities, enabling them to understand, learn, and adapt across multiple domains without the need for explicit programming. Unlike narrow AI, which is limited to performing specific tasks, AGI has the potential to function across various areas of knowledge and problem-solving.

The development of AGI could revolutionise industries such as healthcare, education, finance, and scientific research by surpassing human decision-making capabilities. It promises ground-breaking advancements in personalised medicine, autonomous technologies, and complex data analysis. However, ensuring AGI's safety and alignment with human values is one of the greatest challenges humanity faces. The societal, ethical, and economic implications of AGI are profound and continue to drive intense debates among researchers, policymakers, and ethicists. As we move closer to its realisation, the question of how to harness AGI responsibly becomes increasingly critical.

Why AI-Augmented Creativity?

AI-augmented creativity involves leveraging artificial intelligence to enhance human creative processes in fields such as art, music, design, and writing. By analysing vast datasets and identifying patterns, AI tools like DALL·E, MidJourney, and ChatGPT allow creators to push the boundaries of imagination and innovation. These technologies provide suggestions, generate concepts, and inspire artists to explore creative paths they might never have considered.

AI democratises creativity by empowering individuals without traditional artistic training to produce high-quality works. However, this evolution brings forth thought-provoking questions about originality, intellectual property, and authorship. As AI increasingly collaborates with humans in creative fields, it blurs the line between human ingenuity and machine-assisted production. The challenge lies in finding balance, using AI to enhance, not replace, the creative essence that defines humanity.

Why Sentient AI?

Sentient AI refers to machines that possess the ability to perceive, understand, and potentially experience emotions, much like humans. If achieved, sentient AI could transform the way humans interact with machines, making them more intuitive, empathetic, and responsive. It could revolutionise mental health support, personalised learning environments, and customer service experiences by enabling systems to understand and respond to human emotions on a deeper level.

However, developing sentient AI raises complex ethical and philosophical questions. Should machines with perceived emotions be granted rights? How do we define consciousness and intelligence in a non-biological entity? Pursuing sentient AI challenges humanity's understanding of life itself, pushing the boundaries of technology and morality in unprecedented ways.

Why AI-Powered Personal Assistants?

The future of AI-powered personal assistants goes far beyond setting reminders and managing schedules. These intelligent systems are evolving into proactive life managers that seamlessly integrate into our daily routines. They will be capable of offering hyper-personalised recommendations, managing finances, monitoring health, optimising time, and even anticipating our needs before we articulate them.

Powered by advanced natural language processing and machine learning, these assistants promise to make interactions smooth, intuitive, and natural. However, with this deep integration comes significant concerns about data security and privacy. Striking the right balance between personalisation and safeguarding sensitive information will be critical. As they evolve, AI assistants have the potential to redefine productivity, efficiency, and convenience in the modern world.

Why AI in Predictive Medicine?

AI in predictive medicine leverages advanced algorithms and machine learning techniques to analyse patient data and predict potential health risks before they manifest. By studying medical histories, genetic profiles, and lifestyle information, AI can create personalised treatment plans tailored to individual needs. This proactive approach has the potential to improve patient outcomes significantly, reduce healthcare costs, and enable early interventions.

AI-driven predictive tools also assist in managing large-scale health crises by tracking and forecasting disease outbreaks and identifying public health patterns.

However, challenges remain in ensuring the accuracy of data, protecting patient privacy, and addressing disparities in healthcare access. Despite these obstacles, AI in predictive medicine represents one of the most promising advancements in modern healthcare.

Why Neuromorphic Computing?

Neuromorphic computing is an innovative approach to designing computer systems that mimic the architecture and processes of the human brain. These systems utilize specialised chips that replicate the brain's neural structures, enabling them to process information more efficiently and in parallel. Neuromorphic chips are highly energy-efficient, making them ideal for AI applications in robotics, the Internet of Things (IoT), and autonomous systems.

By significantly reducing power consumption and increasing adaptability, neuromorphic computing pushes the limits of what machines can achieve. It has the potential to revolutionise intelligent systems, making them faster, more responsive, and more human-like in their problem-solving capabilities. Researchers continue to explore scalable hardware and seamless software integration to unlock its full potential, shaping the next generation of computational technology.

Why Brain-Computer Interfaces (BCIs)?

Brain-computer interfaces, or BCIs, are ground-breaking technologies that establish direct communication between the human brain and external devices. By bypassing traditional inputs like keyboards or touchscreens, BCIs enable users to control computers, prosthetics, or other devices using neural signals alone.

This technology holds transformative potential for individuals with disabilities, offering new levels of independence and functionality. For example, BCIs can enable paralyzed individuals to operate robotic limbs or communicate more effectively. Beyond healthcare, BCIs may enhance memory, accelerate learning, and boost cognitive performance in healthy individuals. However, ethical concerns regarding data privacy, consent, and cognitive enhancement remain pressing issues. BCIs challenge our understanding of human-machine integration and raise critical questions about the future of human evolution.

Why AI-Driven Climate Modelling?

AI-driven climate modelling applies advanced algorithms to analyse and predict complex climate systems with unprecedented accuracy. By processing massive datasets from satellites, weather stations, and environmental sensors, AI can forecast extreme weather events, track long-term climate trends, and help policymakers make informed decisions.

This technology identifies the most effective strategies for reducing carbon emissions, adapting to environmental changes, and mitigating the impact of climate change. While AI empowers scientists and decision-makers, its effectiveness depends on data quality, collaboration, and addressing inherent biases in models. AI-driven climate modelling represents a powerful tool for safeguarding the planet and shaping a sustainable future.

Why Quantum AI?

Quantum AI combines the immense power of quantum computing with the adaptability of artificial intelligence, enabling solutions to problems that are beyond the reach of traditional computing systems. Quantum computers process information exponentially faster, making them ideal for solving complex optimisation problems, enhancing cryptography, and running intricate simulations.

Applications of quantum AI span multiple fields, including drug discovery, financial modelling, logistics, and scientific research. However, developing scalable and practical quantum systems remains a significant challenge and the potential misuse of this technology raises ethical and security concerns that must be addressed carefully. Quantum AI represents the next frontier of computational power, offering possibilities that could fundamentally reshape technology and society.

Why AI in Space Exploration?

Artificial intelligence is revolutionising space exploration by automating tasks such as navigation, data analysis, and mission planning. Autonomous rovers and spacecraft use AI to make real-time decisions in distant and challenging environments, reducing reliance on direct human control.

AI also processes vast amounts of data collected from satellites, telescopes, and planetary missions, uncovering insights about the origins and evolution of the universe. By optimising mission efficiency and resource allocation, AI allows scientists to explore deeper into space while minimising risks and costs. As our reliance on AI in space exploration grows, ensuring the safety, adaptability, and reliability of these systems will be critical to the success of future missions.

Chapter 03

Robotics & Automation

Why Digital Twin Technology?

Digital twin technology refers to the creation of virtual replicas of real-world objects, systems, or processes. These replicas act as digital counterparts, allowing businesses and researchers to monitor operations in real time, simulate various scenarios, and optimise performance. By providing an accurate digital representation, this technology helps predict potential outcomes before they occur, reducing risks and preventing costly errors.

Industries such as manufacturing, healthcare, and urban development rely heavily on digital twins to enhance efficiency and decision-making. In smart cities, for instance, digital twins are used to manage traffic, monitor energy consumption, and improve public safety, and they also play a central role in Internet of Things (IoT) integration by linking physical assets with intelligent systems. However, despite their benefits, challenges remain in ensuring precise data accuracy, maintaining cybersecurity, and scaling these systems for large, complex environments.

Why Advanced Robotics?

Advanced robotics represents the fusion of artificial intelligence, machine learning, and state-of-the-art engineering to design robots capable of performing highly complex and precise tasks. These machines are no longer limited to repetitive functions; they now have the capacity to learn, adapt, and make decisions autonomously, transforming industries such as manufacturing, logistics, and healthcare by enhancing productivity, improving accuracy, and reducing workplace hazards.

Robots are now performing intricate surgeries, assembling sophisticated products, and working alongside humans in collaborative environments. Research is also pushing the boundaries toward incorporating emotional intelligence, enabling robots to respond to human needs more naturally. However, as the field advances, ethical considerations – such as job displacement, data privacy, and responsible AI use – continue to drive global discussions.

Why Swarm Robotics?

Swarm robotics takes inspiration from nature, particularly the collective behaviour observed in ant colonies, bee swarms, and bird flocks. It involves multiple robots working together as a unified system to complete tasks that would be difficult or impossible for a single machine. This distributed approach brings immense advantages, including scalability, fault tolerance, and adaptability in unpredictable environments.

Applications range from search-and-rescue missions and disaster recovery operations to agricultural automation and even space exploration. For example, swarms of robots can efficiently cover large areas, gather critical data, and respond quickly to emergencies but the field faces significant challenges, such as achieving seamless communication between units, developing robust coordination algorithms, and ensuring reliable decentralised decision-making.

Why Human Augmentation?

Human augmentation focuses on enhancing human capabilities – physical, cognitive, or sensory by leveraging advanced technologies. This includes innovations like wearable devices, prosthetics, exoskeletons, and even brain-computer interfaces that directly connect our thoughts to machines. Such breakthroughs empower individuals with improved strength, mobility, memory, and perception, reshaping what it means to be human in the technological era.

From restoring lost abilities through prosthetic limbs to enhancing vision with augmented reality, the applications are vast and transformative, but human augmentation also brings significant ethical and societal challenges. Questions arise about equity; who will have access to these enhancements? Privacy concerns grow as personal data becomes deeply intertwined with technology, and debates continue over where to draw the line between natural human evolution and artificial improvement.

Why Hyperloop Technology?

Hyperloop technology proposes a revolutionary mode of transportation, offering ultra-high-speed travel through vacuum-sealed tubes using magnetic levitation. Capable of reaching speeds beyond 700 miles per hour, it promises to drastically reduce travel times between cities, making long-distance commuting more practical than ever before.

Beyond speed, Hyperloop aims to deliver a greener and more energy-efficient alternative to traditional transportation systems, contributing to reduced carbon emissions and sustainable development. However, the path toward implementation faces considerable obstacles, including immense infrastructure costs, safety assurance, and navigating strict regulatory frameworks yet, despite these challenges, its successful realisation could redefine global mobility and reshape how we connect across regions and continents.

Why Autonomous Drones?

Autonomous drones, powered by artificial intelligence and advanced navigation systems, are designed to operate without direct human control. They are widely used across industries for purposes such as parcel delivery, aerial surveillance, agriculture, disaster management, and search-and-rescue missions. By accessing hard-to-reach areas and performing dangerous tasks, drones improve efficiency, reduce operational costs, and save lives in critical situations.

However, the integration of autonomous drones into everyday environments is not without complications. Issues like airspace management, ensuring public safety, maintaining data security, and addressing privacy concerns remain central to large-scale deployment. As technology advances, creating policies and frameworks that balance innovation with responsibility will be key to their success.

Why Zero-Carbon Cities?

Zero-carbon cities aim to achieve net-zero greenhouse gas emissions by incorporating renewable energy, sustainable transportation systems, and intelligent infrastructure. They are envisioned as the future of urban living, addressing urgent challenges posed by climate change and rapid population growth. Through smart technologies, such cities optimise energy use, reduce pollution, and promote healthier lifestyles for their residents.

Yet, building zero-carbon cities involves overcoming several significant hurdles. Developing cost-effective and scalable infrastructure, ensuring equal access to resources, and maintaining long-term sustainability are essential for their viability. While the road is complex, their potential impact on combating global warming and creating environmentally friendly habitats makes them a priority for governments and innovators worldwide.

Why Biodegradable Electronics?

Biodegradable electronics represent a breakthrough in reducing the growing issue of electronic waste by using environmentally friendly materials that naturally decompose after use. These innovations are especially valuable in areas such as medical implants, environmental sensors, and other short-term applications where long-lasting devices are unnecessary or undesirable.

By aligning with global sustainability goals, biodegradable electronics contribute to reducing landfill waste and protecting ecosystems, yet manufacturers face several challenges, including improving device durability, balancing environmental responsibility with performance, and scaling production to meet growing demand. Overcoming these hurdles will be critical to their successful integration into mainstream technology.

Why Energy Harvesting Technologies?

Energy harvesting technologies focus on capturing energy from naturally available sources, such as sunlight, heat, motion, and vibrations, and converting it into usable power. These systems are particularly useful for powering small devices, such as sensors and wearables, where replacing or recharging batteries is impractical.

By reducing reliance on traditional power sources, energy harvesting supports the development of self-sustaining devices and plays a vital role in the Internet of Things (IoT) ecosystem. However, challenges remain in improving conversion efficiency, integrating the technology seamlessly into existing systems, and ensuring cost-effectiveness at scale. As innovations advance, energy harvesting is poised to become a cornerstone of sustainable, low-maintenance technologies.

Why 4D Printing?

4D printing represents an evolution of traditional 3D printing by creating objects and materials capable of changing shape or functionality over time in response to specific triggers, such as temperature, light, or moisture. For example, 4D-printed stents can naturally expand inside blood vessels at body temperature, improving the safety and efficiency of minimally invasive surgeries.

Artificial intelligence enhances 4D printing by optimising material behaviours, predicting transformations, and refining design workflows. In aerospace, this allows for components that can adapt to extreme conditions, while in construction, self-healing materials are developed to automatically repair cracks or adjust to environmental factors like humidity. Even in fashion, AI-driven 4D printing enables fabrics that respond intelligently to body movements and temperature changes. Together, these technologies are shaping a future defined by adaptive, sustainable, and intelligent solutions across multiple industries.

Chapter 04

Advanced Robotics and Automation

Why AI Technology Ethics?

AI technology ethics is becoming increasingly essential because artificial intelligence is now deeply integrated into decision-making processes that profoundly affect human lives. In fields such as healthcare, criminal justice, education, and employment, AI-powered systems are essential with decisions that were once solely made by humans. If these algorithms are not carefully and ethically designed, they can unintentionally perpetuate existing biases, deepen social inequalities, and produce discriminatory outcomes.

For example, AI-driven hiring tools may unintentionally favour certain demographics over others, thereby reinforcing systemic prejudices. Ethical AI design aims to ensure fairness, accountability, and transparency, creating systems that operate without hidden biases and make decisions that can be explained and justified.

Moreover, the rise of AI raises critical concerns surrounding privacy. These systems often collect and analyse massive amounts of personal data, and if mishandled, this information can be misused, potentially infringing upon individuals' rights and freedoms. Another vital aspect of AI ethics is maintaining human oversight, particularly in sensitive domains like healthcare and criminal justice, where autonomous decision-making without accountability could have harmful consequences.

As AI technologies continue to evolve rapidly, ethical guidelines are also needed to address emerging challenges, such as job displacement, deepening economic divides, and the potential for AI misuse in surveillance or military applications. Balancing innovation with human rights is central to ensuring that technological progress aligns with humanity's core values and ultimately, AI ethics serves to build public trust, promote safety, and guarantee that AI-driven systems benefit society as a whole while minimising harm.

Why AI Sustainable Technology?

AI plays a transformative role in driving sustainable technology by optimising processes, reducing waste, and increasing efficiency across multiple sectors. One of its most significant contributions lies in energy management, where AI-powered systems can predict demand patterns and dynamically adjust energy supply. This leads to reduced energy consumption, lower carbon emissions, and a more balanced and efficient energy grid.

In agriculture, AI helps farmers adopt sustainable practices by analysing weather data, soil health, and crop conditions. With these insights, resources like water, fertilizers, and pesticides can be used more precisely, leading to higher yields while protecting the environment. Similarly, AI assists in environmental conservation by monitoring deforestation, tracking pollution levels, and providing real-time data that supports policymakers in crafting effective climate action strategies.

In manufacturing, AI identifies inefficiencies within production lines and helps develop sustainable product designs while minimising material waste. Furthermore, AI supports the integration of renewable energy sources, such as solar and wind power, into existing infrastructure, optimising their contribution to the grid and paving the way for greener energy systems.

AI also influences transportation by aiding the development of electric vehicles, improving autonomous driving systems, and optimising logistics to reduce emissions from supply chains. In smart city initiatives, AI enhances sustainability by managing energy usage, optimising traffic flow, and reducing overall environmental impact. Through these applications, AI is emerging as a powerful catalyst for sustainability, addressing critical environmental challenges and laying the foundation for a cleaner, more resilient future.

Why AI Digital Transformation?

AI stands at the heart of digital transformation, empowering businesses and industries to innovate, streamline operations, and deliver improved customer experiences. By automating repetitive and time-consuming tasks, AI enables organisations to reduce operational costs and free up human talent for more strategic and creative roles.

In customer-facing areas, AI-powered chatbots and virtual assistants provide 24/7 support, improving engagement while minimising response times and operational burdens. Data-driven insights are another cornerstone of AI's contribution to digital transformation. AI systems can analyse massive datasets, extract meaningful patterns, and generate actionable intelligence, helping organisations make well-informed, timely decisions.

In manufacturing, AI optimises production processes, improves product quality, and predicts maintenance needs to prevent costly downtimes. It also drives personalisation in services and marketing by tailoring recommendations, content, and experiences to individual user preferences and behaviours.

Furthermore, AI serves as a bridge between other advanced technologies, such as the Internet of Things (IoT), automation, and smart environments. Whether it's in healthcare, finance, or logistics, AI plays a pivotal role in enhancing diagnostics, improving treatment plans, and streamlining operations. Businesses leveraging AI-driven tools can anticipate market trends, manage risks proactively, and adapt swiftly to changing conditions.

Ultimately, AI-fuelled digital transformation empowers organisations to achieve agility, accelerate innovation, and deliver greater value to customers and stakeholders alike.

Why AI Technology Adoption?

AI technology adoption has become a critical factor for organisations seeking to remain competitive in an increasingly digital-first world. By integrating AI into their operations, businesses can automate routine tasks, streamline complex workflows, and significantly enhance productivity, resulting in measurable cost savings.

AI also enables companies to harness data more effectively, extracting valuable insights for improved decision-making. For example, predictive analytics powered by AI helps organisations forecast market trends, understand customer behaviours, and identify potential risks with greater accuracy.

In manufacturing, AI adoption enhances production efficiency, optimises supply chains, and reduces material waste. In customer engagement, it allows businesses to deliver personalised experiences, offering tailored recommendations and real-time support to build stronger client relationships.

Moreover, AI accelerates innovation by supporting research and development, as it can process vast volumes of information faster than human teams ever could. The integration of AI fosters a culture of continuous improvement, helping organisations remain adaptable in rapidly evolving markets. In essence, adopting AI is not simply about keeping up with technological change; it is about unlocking new growth opportunities, driving operational excellence, and staying ahead in an increasingly competitive landscape.

Why AI Digital Divide?

The AI digital divide refers to the widening gap between individuals, organisations, and nations that have access to AI technologies and those that do not. This divide can deepen social and economic inequalities, as those with access to AI enjoy advantages in education, healthcare, business innovation, and employment opportunities.

Regions or organisations lacking AI infrastructure face significant challenges in implementing advanced solutions, making it harder for them to compete in a technology-driven global economy. Meanwhile, businesses with access to AI can innovate faster, optimise operations, and improve productivity, creating further imbalances.

The divide is also visible in terms of skills. Individuals without opportunities to learn AI-related competencies may find themselves excluded from emerging job markets, worsening existing disparities. In healthcare, unequal access to AI-powered diagnostics can result in vastly different quality of care, leaving underserved populations behind.

Another contributing factor is the unequal distribution of data–the fuel for AI systems. Without access to sufficient, high-quality data, certain regions or institutions struggle to benefit from advancements in AI. Bridging this gap requires targeted efforts, including improving infrastructure, expanding AI education, and ensuring equitable access to resources. Doing so promotes inclusion, fosters innovation, and ensures that AI's benefits are distributed fairly, preventing further fragmentation of society.

Chapter 05

Space and Exploration Technologies

Why Space Tourism?

Space tourism is gradually unlocking an entirely new chapter in human history, offering civilians a chance to experience what was once thought to be accessible only to highly trained astronauts. It provides opportunities for individuals to venture beyond Earth's boundaries and witness the breath-taking beauty of our planet from space. Travelers can enjoy remarkable experiences such as feeling the weightlessness of zero gravity, gazing at stunning orbital views of Earth, and immersing themselves in an environment once considered unattainable.

Companies like SpaceX and Blue Origin are pioneering this industry by developing reusable spacecraft, drastically reducing costs and making space travel more accessible than ever before. Beyond leisure and adventure, space tourism is also driving innovation by fuelling advancements in space technology and exploration. However, several challenges remain, including the need to make these experiences affordable for a wider audience, minimising the environmental impact of launches, and ensuring passenger safety during these extraordinary journeys.

Why Lunar Colonisation?

Lunar colonisation represents one of humanity's most ambitious dreams: establishing permanent human settlements on the Moon. This vision opens doors for extensive scientific research, resource extraction, and deeper space exploration. The Moon's natural resources, such as water ice and regolith, play a critical role in sustaining life by providing essentials like water and oxygen, as well as generating fuel for extended space missions.

By creating a stable human presence on the Moon, we can also use it as a testing ground for technologies designed to colonise other planets in the future. Despite its potential, lunar colonisation faces significant challenges, including the high cost of building infrastructure and the need for robust protection against harmful cosmic radiation. Achieving this vision requires careful planning, technological innovation, and sustained global collaboration.

Why Mars Colonisation?

Mars colonisation envisions the creation of a self-sustaining human civilisation on the Red Planet, presenting humanity with a potential 'second home.' Beyond the excitement of exploration, this mission offers a safeguard for the future of our species in case of catastrophic events on Earth.

Mars is particularly promising due to its available resources, including water ice, and its favourable conditions for harnessing solar power to generate energy. Establishing life there involves developing advanced technologies capable of sustaining human survival under extreme and harsh conditions, such as low temperatures, a thin atmosphere, and radiation exposure.

Alongside technological challenges, there are also important ethical considerations, such as ensuring planetary protection and avoiding irreversible harm to Mars' environment. While the journey is complex, the goal of Mars colonisation represents one of humanity's boldest steps toward interplanetary existence.

Why Space-Based Solar Power?

Space-based solar power (SBSP) offers a revolutionary approach to meeting humanity's growing energy demands by capturing solar energy directly in space and transmitting it wirelessly back to Earth. Unlike terrestrial solar systems, SBSP is unaffected by weather conditions, atmospheric disturbances, or the day-night cycle, making it a consistent and reliable source of clean energy. The potential benefits are vast: as SBSP could provide an uninterrupted energy supply, helping to meet global energy needs sustainably while reducing dependence on fossil fuels.

However, bringing this concept to reality involves overcoming immense technical challenges, including the development of efficient energy transmission methods, constructing large-scale infrastructure in space, and addressing the high costs involved. Despite these obstacles, SBSP stands as a transformative solution for the planet's future energy security.

Why Interstellar Travel Technologies?

Interstellar travel technologies push the boundaries of science and imagination, aiming to make exploration of distant star systems possible. These technologies focus on achieving faster-than-light or near-light-speed travel, enabling humanity to reach beyond our solar system. Innovative concepts such as warp drives, solar sails, and antimatter propulsion are being studied to make interstellar journeys feasible.

The potential outcomes are extraordinary: from discovering habitable planets and alien life to accessing untapped cosmic resources. Yet, these ambitions present profound challenges, as they require breakthroughs in physics, massive technological advancements, and unprecedented financial investment. Interstellar travel forces us to confront the limits of human understanding and challenges us to rethink what is truly possible.

Why Asteroid Mining?

Asteroid mining offers an extraordinary opportunity to extract valuable resources such as rare metals, water, and essential elements from celestial bodies in space. These materials can support space exploration, power future missions, and reduce humanity's reliance on Earth's finite reserves.

Cutting-edge technologies like autonomous robots and AI-driven systems play a central role in identifying, analysing, and extracting these resources efficiently. While asteroid mining has the potential to revolutionise industries both on Earth and beyond, it faces significant hurdles. High operational costs, technological complexity, and unresolved legal questions surrounding the ownership and usage of space resources present ongoing challenges. Nonetheless, the pursuit of asteroid mining marks a major step towards sustaining humanity's long-term presence in space.

Why Space Elevators?

Space elevators propose a ground-breaking alternative to traditional rocket launches, offering a cost-effective and sustainable means of transporting payloads into space. This futuristic concept involves using an ultra-strong tether anchored to Earth that extends far into orbit, enabling vehicles to ascend without the need for rocket propulsion.

If successfully developed, space elevators could revolutionise space exploration by providing frequent, low-cost access to orbit and beyond. Advances in materials science, particularly the development of carbon nanotubes, are essential to making this vision possible. However, several critical challenges remain, including resolving engineering complexities, ensuring safety against potential accidents, and managing the growing issue of orbital debris. While still theoretical, space elevators represent one of the most promising innovations for expanding humanity's reach into space.

Why Cryogenic Technology for Space?

Cryogenic technology is a cornerstone of modern space exploration, enabling the safe storage and transfer of propellants while maintaining spacecraft and equipment at extremely low temperatures. This technology is especially vital for long-duration missions and interplanetary travel, as cryogenic systems preserve essential life-support supplies and stabilize spacecraft under harsh environmental conditions.

Its importance cannot be overstated, as it supports applications ranging from fuelling rockets to protecting sensitive instruments. However, challenges persist in improving energy efficiency, minimising heat loss, and ensuring the reliability of these systems under extreme circumstances. As humanity ventures deeper into space, advancements in cryogenic technology remain critical to mission success.

Why Autonomous Spacecraft?

Autonomous spacecraft represent a leap forward in space exploration, operating independently through advanced AI systems and cutting-edge sensors. By reducing the need for constant human oversight, these spacecrafts can navigate distant or hazardous environments, perform complex analyses, and optimise mission objectives with remarkable efficiency.

From exploring uncharted planets to conducting asteroid studies, autonomous spacecraft expand the possibilities of space research while significantly reducing costs. The development of adaptive, highly reliable systems capable of functioning in extreme space conditions is essential for unlocking the full potential of these technologies.

Why Space-Based Manufacturing?

Space-based manufacturing harnesses the unique advantages of microgravity environments to produce materials and products of exceptional quality that are difficult, or even impossible, to create on Earth. This innovative approach has applications in fields such as advanced pharmaceuticals, semiconductors, and lightweight alloys, enabling breakthroughs that could transform industries.

Furthermore, manufacturing in space reduces the cost and effort of transporting specialised goods from Earth, supporting the development of future space colonies and long-term missions. Despite its potential, scaling up infrastructure and production processes remains a significant challenge. Nonetheless, space-based manufacturing stands at the forefront of innovation, shaping the future of both space exploration and technological progress on Earth.

Chapter 06

The importance of AI in Finance

Why AI in Fraud Detection?

Artificial Intelligence has become a **revolutionary force** in the fight against financial fraud, enabling organisations to identify suspicious activities with unprecedented speed and precision. Traditional fraud detection systems often rely on static rules, but modern financial crimes are dynamic, constantly evolving in sophistication. AI overcomes this challenge by leveraging **machine learning algorithms** capable of analysing **vast volumes of transactional data** in real time.

AI-powered systems can detect **hidden patterns, correlations, and anomalies** that are nearly impossible for human analysts to recognise. Within seconds, they can **flag potentially fraudulent transactions**, enabling institutions to take swift action and minimise financial losses. Furthermore, these systems continuously **learn from historical and real-time data**, improving their accuracy as new fraud techniques emerge.

AI-driven fraud detection tools also reduce **false positives**, ensuring legitimate transactions are not unnecessarily blocked – a key factor in maintaining customer trust and satisfaction. By providing **instant alerts** to both customers and financial institutions, AI helps prevent further damage before fraudulent activities escalate. Additionally, AI improves **operational efficiency** by automating manual monitoring processes, freeing employees to focus on higher-value investigative tasks.

In essence, AI is not just detecting fraud, it is **transforming financial security** by protecting institutions, reducing costs, and strengthening customer confidence.

Why AI in Risk Management?

Risk management in the financial sector has always required a **delicate balance between accuracy and agility**. AI is revolutionising this process by enabling institutions to **identify, assess, and mitigate risks** more effectively than ever before. Through **advanced machine learning models**, AI can analyse **massive datasets** drawn from diverse sources, including market trends, credit behaviour, and geopolitical events, to uncover potential threats before they materialize.

By leveraging **predictive analytics**, AI generates powerful models that simulate **market fluctuations, credit defaults, and systemic risks**, helping businesses make **informed, data-driven decisions** about exposure. These tools also facilitate **real-time monitoring**, enabling financial institutions to respond instantly to sudden market changes or emerging threats.

AI's ability to **evaluate the financial health of companies**, assess credit scores, and analyse industry-specific trends empowers organisations to proactively manage uncertainty. Moreover, AI enhances **stress testing**, simulating multiple 'what-if' scenarios to understand the impact of extreme events on portfolios.

By automating risk-related tasks, AI not only **reduces operational costs** but also **minimises human error**, offering financial institutions a **competitive edge** in an increasingly volatile global market.

Why AI in Algorithmic Trading?

In the **fast-paced world of financial markets**, milliseconds can make the difference between profit and loss. AI plays a **pivotal role** in **algorithmic trading**, allowing financial institutions to execute **faster, smarter, and more precise trades**. By analysing **enormous datasets in real time**, AI-powered algorithms identify **subtle patterns and trends** invisible to human traders.

These systems dynamically **predict market movements**, enabling traders to buy or sell assets at the **most optimal times**. Unlike traditional trading methods, AI models adapt rapidly to **changing market conditions**, continuously refining strategies as they process new information. Importantly, they **eliminate emotional bias**, ensuring that decisions are **purely data-driven**.

AI also manages **large transaction volumes** efficiently, reducing delays and operational bottlenecks. Over time, machine learning models evolve, becoming increasingly **accurate and profitable** as they process more data. For financial institutions, this automation translates into **cost savings, improved efficiency, and higher profitability** while minimising the risks associated with human error.

Simply put, AI has **redefined trading**, turning speed, precision, and adaptability into powerful competitive advantages.

Why AI in Credit Scoring?

Traditional credit scoring models often rely on **limited datasets**, such as repayment history and credit utilization. While effective to a point, these approaches can fail to capture the **full picture of an individual's financial behaviour**. AI **redefines credit scoring** by leveraging **a broader spectrum of data** and applying **advanced machine learning algorithms** to deliver **fairer, faster, and more accurate assessments**.

AI-driven systems analyse **transactional data, spending patterns, social behaviour, and even digital footprints**, uncovering **hidden correlations** between financial habits and credit risk. This allows lenders to assess **borrowers with limited or unconventional credit**

histories, expanding access to financial services for underserved populations.

Furthermore, AI enables **instant credit approvals** by automating the decision-making process, drastically improving customer experience. Its **self-learning capability** ensures that scoring models remain **responsive to evolving economic conditions**, continuously updating their understanding of risk profiles.

By enhancing **accuracy and inclusivity**, AI in credit scoring helps lenders **reduce defaults**, **optimise portfolios**, and **improve profitability**, while giving borrowers a more **transparent and equitable path to credit access**.

Why AI in Customer Service?

Customer service has shifted from being **reactive** to **proactive**, and AI is at the heart of this transformation. Financial institutions now rely on **AI-powered chatbots, virtual assistants, and conversational platforms** to deliver **personalised, efficient, and round-the-clock support**.

AI-driven systems can **instantly resolve routine inquiries** such as balance checks, transaction updates, and loan eligibility, freeing human agents to handle **complex, high-value issues**. Through **predictive analytics**, AI anticipates customer needs, offering **personalised recommendations** for financial products and services.

By continuously **learning from past interactions**, AI becomes better at **understanding context and intent**, resulting in smoother and more **human-like conversations**. It also ensures **omnichannel integration**, providing seamless support across phone, email, chat, and mobile apps.

This **automation** significantly reduces operational costs while **improving response times, customer satisfaction, and loyalty**. With AI, financial institutions can **scale their support services effortlessly** while delivering experiences tailored to individual preferences.

Why AI in Fraud Prevention?

While fraud detection identifies malicious activities **after they occur**, **AI-driven fraud prevention** focuses on

stopping fraudulent transactions before they happen. By continuously monitoring **real-time transactional data**, AI identifies **subtle behavioural anomalies** that traditional systems overlook.

These models analyse **multiple data points simultaneously**, detecting even the most **sophisticated fraud patterns**. Unlike static rule-based systems, AI tools **evolve dynamically**, adapting instantly to **emerging fraud tactics**. Real-time alerts allow financial institutions to **block suspicious transactions immediately**, thereby significantly **reducing financial damage**.

AI also **minimises false positives**, maintaining smooth customer experiences without compromising security. By automating fraud prevention, institutions reduce the need for manual intervention, lowering operational costs and boosting efficiency.

In today's **rapidly evolving digital landscape**, AI acts as a **vigilant guardian**, ensuring financial ecosystems remain secure, trustworthy, and resilient against ever-changing threats.

Why AI in Financial Forecasting?

Accurate forecasting is vital in today's **volatile economic climate**, and AI has become an **indispensable ally** in predicting **market trends and economic shifts**. By processing **massive datasets** from diverse sources, AI uncovers **patterns and relationships** invisible to human analysts.

AI-powered forecasting tools can predict **stock price movements, currency fluctuations, commodity demand, and broader financial indicators** with remarkable precision. They also enable **real-time strategy adjustments**, allowing businesses to capitalise on opportunities and mitigate risks proactively.

Machine learning models improve **continuously** as they ingest new data, resulting in forecasts that become **increasingly reliable over time**. Additionally, AI can simulate **multiple market scenarios**, providing decision-makers with a **comprehensive view of potential outcomes**.

By enhancing **speed, accuracy, and adaptability**, AI-driven financial forecasting empowers organisations to **navigate uncertainty**, **optimise resources**, and make **timely, well-informed decisions**.

Why AI in Investment Management?

Investment management is undergoing a **technological revolution**, with AI enabling **data-driven, personalised, and optimised strategies**. AI algorithms process **historical and real-time data** to identify **hidden opportunities, evaluate risks, and recommend tailored portfolio adjustments**.

These systems automate **routine yet critical tasks**, such as portfolio rebalancing and trade execution, reducing costs and improving operational efficiency. AI also empowers advisors to deliver **customised strategies** aligned with each client's **goals, risk tolerance, and financial aspirations**.

With continuous learning, AI-driven platforms **adapt to market volatility**, enhancing decision-making accuracy and optimising returns. Investors gain **real-time**

insights into their portfolio performance, while institutions leverage predictive models to **anticipate risks and capitalise on emerging trends**.

Ultimately, AI in investment management **democratises sophisticated financial strategies**, enabling both individual and institutional investors to **achieve better outcomes** with **greater confidence and efficiency**.

Why AI in Compliance and Regulation?

Compliance has become increasingly complex as **regulatory frameworks evolve rapidly**. AI provides financial institutions with **powerful tools** to monitor, analyse, and enforce compliance **in real time**.

AI-powered systems streamline **AML (Anti-Money Laundering)**, **KYC (Know Your Customer)**, and other regulatory processes by scanning **massive transactional datasets** for suspicious activities. They **automate reporting**, ensuring institutions meet legal obligations quickly and accurately, thereby reducing the administrative burden on compliance teams.

Machine learning models continuously **adapt to regulatory changes**, helping organisations remain **ahead of emerging threats and requirements**. AI also improves **risk identification**, proactively flagging potential compliance breaches before they escalate into serious issues.

By reducing **manual errors**, accelerating reporting, and enhancing **transparency**, AI ensures institutions maintain **regulatory integrity** while avoiding costly penalties and reputational damage.

Why AI in Wealth Management?

Wealth management is increasingly shifting toward **personalisation and data-driven insights**, and AI is at the forefront of this transformation. By analysing **large datasets**, AI uncovers **investment trends, opportunities, and risks** that human advisors might miss.

AI-driven platforms craft **customised portfolios** aligned with each client's **objectives, preferences, and risk tolerance**. They continuously **monitor portfolio performance in real time**, automatically adjusting strategies to optimise returns.

Clients benefit from **greater transparency and control**, accessing **real-time insights** into their investments, while advisors leverage AI-powered recommendations to **deliver proactive guidance**, enhancing both trust and client satisfaction.

By automating repetitive tasks, AI **reduces operational costs** and empowers wealth managers to focus on **strategic decision-making**. Ultimately, AI in wealth management **enhances personalisation, improves returns, and strengthens client relationships** in a rapidly evolving financial landscape.

Chapter 07

The Next Generation Use of AI

Why Next-Generation AI in Healthcare?

Next-generation Artificial Intelligence (AI) is reshaping the healthcare industry by introducing ground-breaking advancements in diagnostics, treatment, and operational efficiency. With the power of advanced algorithms, AI can process massive volumes of complex medical data, including diagnostic images, genomic information, and patient records, within seconds enabling faster decision-making. These systems are capable of identifying intricate patterns and correlations that often go unnoticed by the human eye, enabling early detection of diseases and more accurate diagnoses.

AI-powered predictive models are becoming invaluable to doctors, as they can forecast potential health issues long before symptoms become visible, allowing for preventive measures and timely interventions. By analysing vast datasets, AI generates insights into disease mechanisms, treatment responses, and drug efficacy, helping doctors make more informed clinical decisions.

One of the most remarkable aspects of next-generation AI is its ability to continuously learn and improve. With every data point processed, AI systems become smarter and more precise over time, making them increasingly reliable in assisting medical professionals. Surgeons benefit from AI-driven tools that enhance surgical accuracy, reduce the likelihood of complications, and support decision-making during complex procedures.

Moreover, AI accelerates the drug discovery process by predicting molecular interactions and potential drug responses, significantly reducing the time and cost required to bring new medicines to market. Beyond diagnosis and treatment, AI optimises hospital resource allocation, streamlines workflows, and improves operational efficiency thereby enhancing overall healthcare delivery. These advancements make healthcare more affordable, accessible, and effective.

Overall, next-generation AI in healthcare improves patient outcomes, enhances safety, reduces costs, and raises the overall quality of care, making it one of the most transformative forces in modern medicine.

Why Next-Generation AI in Education?

Next-generation AI is revolutionising education by creating personalised, adaptive, and highly effective learning experiences for students. Unlike traditional teaching methods that adopt a uniform approach, AI-powered adaptive learning systems assess each student's strengths, weaknesses, and learning pace, and adjust coursework and teaching methods accordingly. This ensures that every learner progresses based on their individual capabilities.

AI-based tools provide immediate, real-time feedback to students, helping them identify areas where improvement is needed while reinforcing concepts they've already mastered. Virtual AI tutors are available beyond regular classroom hours, offering continuous support and answering questions whenever required, thus fostering self-paced learning and independence.

Machine learning algorithms analyse student data to predict performance outcomes and recommend tailored strategies for improvement. Educators also benefit as AI streamlines time-consuming administrative tasks, such as grading assignments, tracking attendance, and preparing reports, enabling them to focus more on teaching and student engagement.

AI-powered platforms make educational content more interactive, engaging, and accessible, accommodating diverse learning needs and styles. The technology also promotes inclusive education by supporting students with disabilities and catering to varied cognitive abilities.

Furthermore, AI enables seamless remote learning, ensuring access to quality education regardless of geographical location. Overall, next-generation AI is reshaping the educational landscape by fostering inclusivity, boosting engagement, improving efficiency, and providing a more tailored learning experience for every student.

Why Next-Generation AI in Manufacturing?

Next-generation AI is transforming the manufacturing industry by driving higher productivity, improving quality control, and enabling predictive maintenance. AI-powered systems continuously monitor production lines in real time, detecting inefficiencies, defects, and irregularities that could affect output quality or disrupt operations.

Through predictive maintenance, AI analyses equipment data to forecast potential failures before they occur, thereby minimising unplanned downtime and significantly reducing repair costs. AI-guided automation also enhances precision, speed, and consistency during production, resulting in faster manufacturing cycles and improved product reliability.

Inventory management becomes more efficient with AI as it predicts demand accurately and adjusts stock levels accordingly, reducing waste and optimising resource allocation. Advanced algorithms analyse production data to identify patterns and streamline workflows, ensuring smooth and efficient manufacturing operations.

AI-driven systems improve product quality by identifying even the smallest anomalies that may escape human inspection, guaranteeing higher standards and customer satisfaction. Furthermore, AI enhances supply chain resilience by predicting potential disruptions and suggesting preventive measures to ensure timely deliveries.

By optimising energy consumption and minimising material waste, AI also supports sustainability initiatives within manufacturing. In short, next-generation AI empowers manufacturers to produce higher-quality goods faster and at lower costs, all while maintaining greater operational efficiency and environmental responsibility.

Why Next-Generation AI in Retail?

Next-generation AI is redefining the retail landscape by revolutionising customer experiences, streamlining inventory processes, and optimising sales strategies. AI-driven recommendation engines analyse customer preferences, shopping behaviour, and browsing history to deliver highly personalised product suggestions, increasing customer satisfaction and driving higher conversion rates.

Machine learning algorithms allow retailers to predict demand accurately, ensuring optimal stock availability and reducing the risks of overstocking or stockouts. AI-powered chatbots provide round-the-clock customer support, responding instantly to queries, resolving concerns, and improving throughout the shopping journey.

AI also enables retailers to analyse customer feedback and purchasing patterns, which helps fine-tune product offerings and adapt marketing strategies to evolving consumer preferences. By studying market trends and competitor pricing, AI improves pricing strategies, ensuring competitiveness and profitability.

In physical stores, AI-driven innovations like cashier-less checkouts, smart shelves, and interactive displays enhance the shopping experience while streamlining operations. Accurate inventory forecasting reduces waste, optimises supply chain management, and ensures smoother workflows.

Additionally, AI-powered analytics track customer sentiment and purchasing trends, allowing retailers to refine marketing campaigns and product development strategies effectively. Overall, next-generation AI in retail boosts operational efficiency, enhances customer engagement, maximises profitability, and creates seamless shopping experiences across both digital and physical channels.

Why Next-Generation AI in Finance?

Next-generation AI is reshaping the financial sector by revolutionising decision-making, fraud detection, and investment strategies. AI-powered systems process vast amounts of financial data in real time to identify patterns, predict market fluctuations, and optimise investment portfolios for better returns.

AI enhances risk management by evaluating potential threats and providing financial institutions with actionable insights so they can make informed decisions.

In fraud detection, AI systems analyse transaction data continuously, flagging unusual activities instantly and preventing financial crimes with unprecedented accuracy.

By incorporating broader data points, AI improves credit scoring, enabling more precise assessments of borrowers' creditworthiness and expanding financial access to a larger population. Automated trading platforms powered by AI execute transactions faster than human traders, adjusting strategies in real time to capitalise on market trends.

Routine tasks such as document verification, compliance checks, and reporting are automated, reducing operational costs and freeing financial professionals to focus on strategic planning. Additionally, AI-powered personalisation allows banks and financial firms to deliver tailored recommendations, investment options, and products to individual clients.

AI-driven financial forecasting tools provide businesses with accurate projections of future outcomes, helping organisations prepare for changing economic conditions. In essence, next-generation AI in finance improves efficiency, strengthens security, minimises risks, and delivers enhanced customer experiences while driving overall growth in the financial sector.

Why Next-Generation AI in Energy?

Next-generation AI is revolutionising the energy sector by improving efficiency, promoting sustainability, and optimising grid management. AI-powered systems monitor energy usage in real time, identifying consumption patterns and minimising waste while lowering operational costs.

Machine learning models forecast energy demand accurately, enabling utility providers to manage supply effectively and prevent outages. AI plays a critical role in renewable energy advancements by enhancing energy storage systems, optimising wind and solar power generation, and reducing dependence on fossil fuels.

Smart grids, powered by AI, automatically balance energy loads and distribute resources where they are needed most, improving overall energy reliability and stability. AI-driven predictive maintenance ensures that potential equipment failures are identified and addressed before they cause disruptions, reducing downtime and repair expenses.

By analysing weather patterns and environmental data, AI predicts peak renewable energy production times, helping companies maximise efficiency and output. These technologies also support sustainability goals by enabling organisations to lower carbon emissions and transition toward cleaner energy solutions.

Additionally, AI accelerates research and development within the energy sector by driving innovation and developing technologies to meet the rising global energy demand. Ultimately, next-generation AI in energy ensures a more efficient, resilient, and environmentally responsible energy future.

Why Next-Generation AI in Transportation?

Next-generation AI is transforming transportation by enhancing safety, efficiency, and sustainability across various modes of travel. Autonomous vehicles, powered by AI, are capable of navigating roads safely, interpreting traffic signals, and avoiding collisions, thereby reducing the need for human intervention and minimising accidents.

AI-driven traffic management systems analyse real-time data to optimise traffic flow, reduce congestion, and shorten travel times in urban areas. In logistics, AI-powered route optimisation minimises fuel consumption, lowers operational costs, and ensures faster delivery timelines.

Predictive maintenance in transportation infrastructure, enabled by AI, identifies potential faults in roads, vehicles, and systems before they cause delays or failures. Machine learning models also predict traffic patterns and adjust public transportation schedules to meet demand more effectively, ensuring smoother commutes.

AI supports the development of smart cities by integrating transportation systems with real-time data streams to enhance mobility solutions. In aviation, AI optimises flight schedules, monitors air traffic, and improves operational safety and efficiency.

Furthermore, AI-powered vehicles and systems are improving fuel efficiency, reducing greenhouse gas emissions, and supporting environmentally sustainable practices. Overall, next-generation AI in transportation is creating smarter, safer, and more eco-friendly mobility solutions that cater to the evolving demands of modern society.

Why Next-Generation AI in Agriculture?

Next-generation AI is revolutionising agriculture by improving crop management, increasing yields, and promoting sustainable farming practices. AI-powered systems analyse soil composition, weather data, and crop health to provide actionable insights that help farmers make smarter decisions.

Machine learning algorithms predict optimal planting times, irrigation schedules, and harvesting windows, ensuring maximum productivity and resource efficiency. AI-enabled drones and sensors monitor farmlands in real time, detecting pest infestations, soil deficiencies, or disease outbreaks early, allowing for targeted and timely interventions.

Through precision farming, AI integrates data from multiple sources to optimise the use of resources such as water, fertilisers, and pesticides, reducing waste and environmental impact. Additionally, AI streamlines agricultural supply chains, minimising food waste and ensuring timely delivery from farms to markets.

AI also supports sustainable farming practices by promoting eco-friendly cultivation techniques and helping farmers adapt to changing environmental conditions. Predictive analytics assist in managing risks related to climate change, extreme weather events, and fluctuating market demands.

By automating routine tasks like monitoring, planting, and harvesting, AI frees farmers to focus on strategic decision-making. Ultimately, next-generation AI in agriculture enhances food security, boosts productivity, and fosters sustainable farming for future generations.

Why Next-Generation AI in Cybersecurity?

Next-generation AI is reshaping cybersecurity by providing faster, more accurate, and proactive threat detection and response mechanisms. AI-powered systems continuously monitor network traffic, detecting unusual patterns or anomalies that may indicate cyberattacks or breaches.

By leveraging machine learning, these systems learn from previous attacks, constantly improving their ability to identify emerging threats. AI enables real-time responses to security risks, significantly reducing the potential damage caused by malicious activities and data breaches.

AI-driven tools also automate routine security operations such as vulnerability scans, patch management, and system updates, allowing cybersecurity professionals to focus on higher-level strategic tasks while predictive analytics powered by AI forecast potential attack vectors, helping organisations implement preventive measures before threats materialise.

Incident response times are greatly improved as AI systems can quickly pinpoint the source of breaches and provide effective mitigation strategies. These solutions also reduce false positives, ensuring security teams focus their resources on genuine threats.

Overall, next-generation AI in cybersecurity strengthens defences, enhances organisational resilience, mitigates risks, and delivers robust protection against an ever-evolving landscape of cyber threats.

Why Next-Generation AI in Smart Cities?

Next-generation AI plays a critical role in developing smart cities, transforming urban living through efficient resource management and improved infrastructure. AI-powered systems analyse real-time data to optimise traffic flows, reduce congestion, and shorten commuting times.

In energy management, AI ensures a balance between supply and demand while reducing waste and supporting sustainability initiatives. AI-enabled smart sensors monitor essential city functions such as air quality, water usage, and waste management, ensuring smooth and efficient operations.

Predictive analytics help city planners make informed decisions on infrastructure development, accounting for population growth and evolving urban needs. AI also enhances public safety through intelligent surveillance systems capable of detecting anomalies and potential threats in real time, while emergency response is improved as AI predicts incidents, allocates resources effectively, and ensures rapid deployment of first responders. Additionally, AI-enabled solutions improve public transportation by optimising routes, managing schedules, and making services more accessible to citizens.

By enhancing citizen engagement, providing real-time updates on infrastructure and services, and supporting sustainability goals, next-generation AI in smart cities elevates the overall quality of life, creating more efficient, safe, and environmentally responsible urban environments designed for the future.

Chapter 08

AI-Power Drone

(Fast, Efficient, and Autonomous)

Why AI in Drone Navigation?

AI in drone navigation enhances accuracy and efficiency in autonomous flight. Advanced algorithms enable drones to map and navigate environments in real time, avoiding obstacles and adjusting their paths seamlessly. AI supports GPS-free navigation by using visual and sensor data, making it possible for drones to operate in challenging environments like urban areas or indoors.

Machine learning allows drones to adapt to new surroundings, learn flight paths, and create maps without human intervention. With AI, drones can plan optimal routes while considering weather conditions, terrain, and obstacles, ensuring smooth and collision-free flights. By continuously analysing data from cameras, LIDAR, and radar sensors, AI-driven drones make split-second decisions that improve safety and reliability.

AI-powered navigation reduces human error, boosts operational efficiency, and enables drones to respond to unexpected environmental changes, ensuring mission success.

Why AI in Drone Surveillance?

AI-powered drones are transforming surveillance by offering advanced monitoring and analysis capabilities. Using real-time data, these drones autonomously detect unusual activity or security threats. AI-driven image recognition algorithms allow drones to identify faces, vehicles, and objects of interest, improving surveillance precision.

Machine learning enables drones to analyse vast datasets, detect behavioural patterns, and generate actionable insights. They can automatically patrol designated areas, adjusting flight paths to optimise coverage. With AI, drones can track moving objects, monitor high-security zones, and oversee large-scale events effectively.

In search and rescue scenarios, AI-powered drones quickly locate missing persons or detect heat signatures. By distinguishing between threats and non-threats in real time, they enhance response times while reducing the need for extensive manpower. Overall, AI in drone surveillance enables continuous, high-precision monitoring, improving security and safety.

Why AI in Drone Delivery?

AI revolutionises drone delivery by optimising flight paths for efficient and safe operations. Machine learning algorithms help drones analyse traffic, weather, and terrain to determine the fastest and most fuel-efficient routes. AI-powered drones automatically adjust their course to avoid obstacles, navigate urban areas, and deliver packages accurately.

Real-time AI systems predict potential delays or hazards and adapt routes instantly to ensure timely deliveries. These drones can track packages, verify addresses, and reduce human error, improving delivery accuracy. AI also enhances performance in adverse weather conditions and optimises battery usage for longer flight times and sustainability.

By learning from past delivery data, AI systems continuously improve strategies, reducing costs and increasing customer satisfaction. AI makes drone deliveries faster, safer, and more reliable, paving the way for the future of logistics.

Why AI in Drone Agriculture?

AI-powered drones are transforming agriculture by delivering precise, data-driven insights into crop health. Equipped with multispectral cameras, these drones detect pests, diseases, and nutrient deficiencies with high accuracy. AI algorithms process this data to provide actionable insights, enabling farmers to make informed decisions about irrigation, fertilisation, and pest control.

Drones autonomously survey large farmlands, collecting high-resolution images and mapping areas needing attention. AI predicts crop yields by analysing growth patterns, soil conditions, and weather factors, helping farmers optimise resource usage and reduce waste.

By automating repetitive tasks like monitoring fields or applying fertilisers, AI drones improve efficiency, enhance crop quality, and promote sustainable farming practices. Overall, AI in agriculture empowers farmers to increase productivity while reducing environmental impact.

Why AI in Drone Inspection?

AI-driven drones are revolutionising inspections across industries like energy, construction, and infrastructure. Using AI algorithms, drones analyse images and sensor data to detect wear, damage, or faults in structures such as bridges, pipelines, and power lines.

These drones perform routine inspections autonomously, identifying potential risks and providing detailed reports. In power line inspections, AI helps pinpoint defects that could cause outages, allowing for preventative maintenance. By eliminating the need for manual inspections in hazardous or hard-to-reach areas, AI improves worker safety and reduces operational costs.

AI also optimises flight paths, enabling drones to cover larger areas faster and more efficiently. Overall, AI in drone inspections ensures greater accuracy, safety, and efficiency.

Why AI in Drone Search and Rescue?

AI significantly enhances drone capabilities in search and rescue missions. Drones powered by AI rapidly scan vast, hard-to-reach areas such as mountains, forests, and disaster zones. Advanced algorithms process visual data to detect survivors by recognising movement, heat signatures, or specific patterns.

AI enables drones to autonomously navigate rugged terrains and adjust flight paths in real time. Equipped with thermal cameras, infrared sensors, and video feeds, AI-driven drones locate missing persons, identify hazards, and deliver medical supplies when necessary.

Through continuous learning, AI systems improve drone performance, making them more efficient over time. By accelerating response times and boosting success rates, AI-powered drones are revolutionising emergency search and rescue operations and saving lives.

Why AI in Drone Traffic Management?

AI in drone traffic management is essential for maintaining safety and efficiency as drone usage grows. AI-powered systems track and manage drone movements, preventing collisions and ensuring optimal flight paths.

By processing real-time data, AI predicts airspace congestion, suggests alternate routes, and accounts for weather, no-fly zones, and aerial obstacles. It enables seamless coordination among multiple drones operating in the same airspace, maintaining safe distances and preventing disruptions.

In emergencies, AI can prioritise drone routes, allowing critical missions to proceed without delays. Automating traffic management reduces reliance on human intervention, making large-scale drone operations safer and more scalable.

Why AI in Drone Environmental Monitoring?

AI-powered drones play a crucial role in monitoring ecosystems and wildlife. By collecting data on temperature, pollution levels, vegetation health, and water quality, these drones help track environmental changes and predict potential risks such as climate change effects or habitat destruction.

AI processes data to detect pollution hotspots, monitor illegal activities like deforestation, and track wildlife populations. In marine environments, AI-equipped drones measure water quality and identify harmful algal blooms.

By enabling continuous, large-scale monitoring, AI supports informed decision-making, disaster recovery efforts, and sustainability initiatives. Overall, AI-driven environmental monitoring ensures accurate, real-time insights for better conservation strategies.

Why AI in Drone Agriculture Pest Control?

AI-powered drones are redefining pest control in agriculture with precise, targeted solutions. These drones autonomously patrol fields, using machine learning to detect early signs of infestations, such as unusual crop damage patterns.

AI algorithms identify specific pest species, assess infestation severity, and guide farmers to apply pesticides only where needed, reducing environmental harm. Drones can also release beneficial insects or apply organic treatments with pinpoint accuracy, minimising chemical use.

By monitoring pest populations over time, AI helps farmers develop effective long-term control strategies. Real-time decision-making enables faster responses, improving crop yields and promoting sustainable farming practices.

Why AI in Drone Fleet Management?

AI in drone fleet management enables companies to control and monitor multiple drones efficiently. AI algorithms optimise flight paths, scheduling, and resource allocation, ensuring maximum productivity.

Real-time monitoring provides insights into drone locations, battery levels, and operational status. AI anticipates potential issues, such as battery depletion or maintenance needs, automatically redistributing drones to meet demand.

By analysing data from past missions, AI systems refine future operations, improving efficiency and reducing downtime. With enhanced safety measures and predictive analytics, AI-driven fleet management streamlines drone operations, scales capacity, and lowers costs.

Chapter 09

AI Autonomous Car

Why AI is Crucial for Autonomous Car Navigation?

AI is the backbone of autonomous car navigation, enabling vehicles to handle complex environments seamlessly. Using **machine learning** and advanced algorithms, AI analyses vast amounts of **real-time data** from cameras, sensors, and radar to understand road conditions, obstacles, and traffic.

AI systems detect pedestrians, cyclists, vehicles, and lane markings with high accuracy, ensuring **safe and smooth travel without human intervention**. Unlike humans, AI processes information faster and more precisely, making it indispensable for **real-time decision-making**.

Additionally, AI enables **predictive analysis**, anticipating potential hazards and taking **preventive actions** to avoid collisions. The system continuously learns from new data, improving its performance over time and adapting to dynamic environments.

By recognising **traffic signals, road signs, and lane boundaries**, AI ensures **seamless navigation** while eliminating human errors – one of the major causes of accidents. With AI at the core, autonomous driving delivers **enhanced safety, efficiency, and comfort**, setting the foundation for the future of self-driving technology.

Why AI Improves Autonomous Car Safety?

AI significantly improves the safety of autonomous vehicles by providing a **360-degree environmental view** and **instant situational awareness**. Machine learning models are trained to **detect objects**, **predict motion patterns**, and **analyse driving conditions**, enabling faster and more accurate responses than human drivers.

AI evaluates **risk levels in real time**, reacting swiftly to **sudden lane changes**, **pedestrians crossing**, or **unexpected obstacles**. It supports advanced **collision-avoidance systems** that prevent accidents before they occur.

By **reducing human errors**, the leading cause of road accidents, AI makes driving safer for everyone. Moreover, autonomous cars equipped with AI can **communicate with other vehicles and infrastructure** to further improve traffic safety.

AI also powers **advanced driver-assistance systems (ADAS),** like lane-keeping assistance, adaptive cruise control, and automatic emergency braking. By combining predictive capabilities with proactive measures, AI ensures **safer roads** and protects both passengers and pedestrians.

Why AI Enables Efficient Traffic Management in Autonomous Cars?

AI plays a vital role in **optimising urban traffic flow** by allowing autonomous cars to communicate through **vehicle-to-vehicle (V2V)** and **vehicle-to-infrastructure (V2I)** systems. This seamless communication enables cars to **synchronise movements**, **reduce congestion**, and **improve overall efficiency**.

AI systems **analyse real-time traffic data**, detect **accidents or road closures**, and dynamically reroute vehicles to avoid bottlenecks. By predicting **congestion hotspots**, AI suggests **alternate paths** and ensures vehicles maintain **optimal speeds** at intersections and traffic lights.

Through better coordination, AI minimises **travel time**, **reduces fuel consumption**, and lowers **emissions**. Accurate **arrival-time predictions** also improve ride planning and passenger satisfaction.

In the long term, AI-driven **traffic management systems** will make transportation **more sustainable, efficient, and environmentally friendly**, shaping the future of **smart urban mobility**.

Why AI Supports Autonomous Car Decision-Making?

Autonomous vehicles rely on AI for **split-second decision-making** in complex driving scenarios. By **processing sensor and camera data**, AI continuously evaluates surroundings, detecting **other vehicles**, **pedestrians**, and **unexpected obstacles**.

Machine learning models are trained to **recognise patterns** and **predict future events**, helping cars make **data-driven decisions** based on likely outcomes. In emergencies, AI determines the safest response, whether to **brake, swerve, or accelerate**, in just milliseconds.

Over time, AI **learns and adapts** to new driving environments, improving its **decision-making capabilities**. From **navigating crowded intersections** to **handling unpredictable pedestrian behaviour**, AI ensures safer, faster, and more reliable driving choices.

By removing **human biases** and emotional influences, AI enables **objective and precise judgements**, ultimately making autonomous vehicles **safer and more dependable**.

Why AI Enhances Autonomous Car Comfort and User Experience?

AI elevates the **comfort and personalisation** of autonomous vehicles by adapting to passenger preferences and creating a **customised travel experience**.

AI-powered systems automatically adjust **seat positions**, **climate controls**, and **entertainment options** based on individual user profiles. Through **natural language processing (NLP)**, passengers can interact with the vehicle using **voice commands**, enabling effortless hands-free control.

AI also anticipates passenger needs, such as **suggesting entertainment**, **adjusting lighting**, or **modifying cabin temperature** during long trips. Advanced **AI-driven suspension systems** enhance ride quality by adapting to road conditions for smoother journeys.

Additionally, AI can **detect passenger moods**, activating features like **relaxation modes** or **stress-reducing sounds** to enhance the travel experience. By optimising **routes** and reducing **travel time**, AI ensures passengers enjoy **efficient, comfortable, and personalised rides**.

Why AI Enhances Autonomous Car Efficiency?

AI significantly boosts the **efficiency** of autonomous vehicles by optimising **routes**, **energy usage**, and **driving behaviour**.

Machine learning algorithms process **real-time traffic data** to calculate the **most efficient routes**, avoiding congestion and delays. Autonomous cars powered by AI automatically adjust speeds to **reduce fuel consumption** and **minimise energy waste**.

For **electric vehicles (EVs)**, AI maximises **battery performance** by managing power usage and predicting optimal charging points. Through **predictive maintenance**, AI detects potential issues early, reducing downtime and costly repairs.

By continuously monitoring **vehicle performance** and adjusting systems like **engine, braking, and acceleration**, AI ensures **smarter energy use** and **longer vehicle lifespan**, making transportation more **sustainable and cost-effective**.

Why AI Improves Autonomous Car Security?

AI strengthens **security** in autonomous vehicles by integrating advanced **threat-detection** and **cybersecurity mechanisms**.

AI-powered surveillance systems monitor surroundings to identify **potential threats**, such as **suspicious activity** or **road hazards**. Machine learning algorithms analyse vehicle movement patterns, enabling the car to **predict and respond** to **aggressive driving** or **potential collisions** in real time.

Additionally, AI safeguards autonomous cars against **cyberattacks** by deploying **real-time encryption systems** and protecting sensitive passenger data from breaches. Integration with **external security infrastructure**, such as cameras and sensors, enhances situational awareness and **vehicle tracking**, making it easier to recover stolen cars.

By combining **physical safety** with **digital protection**, AI ensures that autonomous vehicles remain **secure on the road and online**.

Why AI Supports Autonomous Car Environmental Impact Reduction?

AI contributes to **sustainable transportation** by reducing the **environmental footprint** of autonomous vehicles.

AI optimises **driving patterns**, ensuring smoother acceleration and braking to **lower fuel consumption** and **reduce emissions**. When paired with **electric vehicles**, AI extends **battery range** and minimises **energy waste**, making eco-friendly driving more efficient.

Machine learning systems also predict **maintenance needs**, preventing **inefficient operations** and extending vehicle lifespan. By choosing **shorter, congestion-free routes**, AI cuts **carbon emissions** and decreases **urban air pollution**.

Through smarter **traffic-flow management**, AI reduces **idling times**, enabling greener cities and cleaner air. As autonomous cars become widespread, AI will play a **key role** in developing **sustainable, eco-friendly transportation ecosystems**.

Why AI Accelerates Autonomous Car Adoption and Integration?

AI speeds up the **adoption and integration** of autonomous vehicles by making them **safer, smarter, and more reliable**.

With improved algorithms, autonomous cars can **handle complex environments** and **adverse conditions** more effectively, building **public trust** in self-driving technology.

AI ensures **seamless integration** with **smart infrastructure**, such as **intelligent traffic lights**, **connected roads**, and **digital signage**, resulting in smoother operations.

By continuously **learning and adapting**, AI makes autonomous vehicles more capable while **reducing operational costs**, driving **widespread acceptance** and paving the way for a **fully autonomous transportation future**.

Why AI and Human-Machine Collaboration in Autonomous Cars is Key?

AI bridges the gap between **human intuition** and **machine precision**, enabling **seamless collaboration** between passengers and vehicles.

Autonomous cars allow drivers to stay engaged when needed, with AI **assisting in complex scenarios** and providing **real-time feedback** to avoid potential risks. Passengers can interact with AI-powered systems through **intuitive interfaces** and **voice commands** for effortless control.

AI learns from **passenger preferences**, adjusting settings like **seating**, **entertainment**, and **climate control** to create a **personalised experience**.

In **mixed traffic environments**, AI ensures **clear communication** between humans and machines, helping drivers make **informed decisions** when manual intervention is required.

As AI evolves, **human-machine collaboration** will become essential for the **safe, efficient, and enjoyable operation** of autonomous cars.

Chapter 10

Sustainable and Green Technologies

Why AI is Vital for the Future of Renewable Energy?

Artificial Intelligence plays a critical role in shaping the future of renewable energy by optimising energy generation, distribution, and storage. Machine learning algorithms analyse vast amounts of data from sources like solar, wind, and hydropower systems to forecast energy production with remarkable accuracy. These predictions allow energy providers to manage power grids more effectively, balancing supply and demand to minimise waste and avoid shortages.

AI-driven smart grids can automatically adjust energy flows based on real-time usage patterns, ensuring that renewable energy is utilised efficiently and sustainably. Predictive analytics further enhance reliability by identifying maintenance needs in solar panels, wind turbines, and other infrastructure before failures occur, reducing downtime and repair costs.

Additionally, AI optimises energy storage by determining the best times to store excess energy and release it when demand is high, helping integrate renewables seamlessly into existing power systems. These intelligent systems improve operational efficiency, lower costs, and reduce our reliance on fossil fuels.

By supporting large-scale renewable integration, AI accelerates the transition to a low-carbon economy and contributes directly to global sustainability goals. In essence, AI is indispensable for achieving a greener, more sustainable energy future.

Why AI Enhances Sustainability in Smart Cities?

AI plays a transformative role in building sustainable smart cities by improving the efficiency of urban systems and minimising environmental impact. Intelligent AI-powered platforms optimise critical infrastructure, including transportation, waste management, and energy consumption, to make cities cleaner and more efficient.

AI-driven traffic management systems monitor real-time vehicle flow, adjust signal timings dynamically, and suggest alternative routes, effectively reducing congestion and lowering carbon emissions. In waste management, AI-powered systems ensure efficient collection, sorting, and recycling, decreasing landfill usage and promoting a circular economy.

Energy consumption is also optimised through AI-managed smart grids, which analyse real-time demand and distribute power accordingly, reducing unnecessary energy waste. AI technologies predict consumption patterns, helping city planners design long-term sustainable growth strategies.

Moreover, AI-enabled environmental monitoring tools track air quality, noise levels, and pollution sources, enabling faster interventions to protect public health. AI-integrated building management systems further improve sustainability by intelligently controlling heating, cooling, and lighting to reduce energy consumption.

By facilitating renewable energy adoption and enhancing overall resource efficiency, AI empowers cities to become more resilient, eco-friendly, and adaptive to the challenges of rapid urbanisation.

Why AI Promotes Sustainable Agriculture?

AI is revolutionising agriculture by enabling sustainable farming practices that enhance productivity while conserving resources and protecting the environment. Through precision farming technologies, AI-powered sensors, drones, and satellite imagery continuously monitor soil conditions, crop health, weather patterns, and pest activity in real-time.

Machine learning algorithms process this data to recommend optimal planting schedules, crop rotations, and fertiliser use, improving yields while minimising waste. AI-driven irrigation systems adjust water usage automatically, ensuring crops receive the right amount without unnecessary consumption, which is especially crucial in regions facing water scarcity.

Furthermore, AI enhances pest and disease management by detecting early outbreaks and enabling targeted treatment, significantly reducing the need for widespread pesticide use. Smart farming equipment powered by AI even allows farmers to monitor individual plants and deliver personalised care for maximum efficiency.

AI also plays a vital role in developing climate-resilient crop varieties by analysing genetic data and simulating environmental stress conditions, ensuring food security amid changing climates. By optimising supply chains and reducing food waste, AI contributes to lowering agriculture's carbon footprint.

Ultimately, AI supports a sustainable agricultural ecosystem by conserving resources, improving efficiency, and securing long-term global food supplies.

How AI is Advancing Waste Management and Recycling?

AI is redefining waste management and recycling by introducing advanced automation and predictive capabilities that make these systems smarter, faster, and more sustainable. AI-powered sorting systems use computer vision and robotics to separate recyclables from non-recyclables with precision levels far exceeding human capabilities.

Machine learning algorithms analyse waste generation patterns to predict future volumes, enabling municipalities to optimise collection schedules, reduce unnecessary pickups, and cut emissions from waste transportation. Smart bins equipped with AI sensors monitor fill levels and automatically request collection when required, further improving efficiency.

In recycling plants, AI-driven robotic arms identify, sort, and process materials rapidly, improving throughput and ensuring higher-quality recycled outputs. AI also detects contamination in recycling streams, enhancing the purity and reusability of recovered materials.

Additionally, AI-driven analytics help designers adopt sustainable product lifecycles by creating products meant for disassembly and reuse, promoting a circular economy. AI technologies are even advancing innovative upcycling solutions, transforming discarded materials into valuable products.

By integrating AI into waste management and recycling systems, cities and industries can significantly reduce landfill dependency, conserve natural resources, and lower environmental impact.

Why AI for Carbon Footprint Reduction in Manufacturing?

AI plays a transformative role in helping manufacturers reduce their carbon footprint and transition to greener production methods. By monitoring equipment performance and energy consumption in real-time, AI-powered systems optimise production processes to minimise energy waste and emissions.

Machine learning models predict equipment maintenance needs before breakdowns occur, ensuring machines operate at peak efficiency and reducing unnecessary downtime. In supply chain management, AI identifies opportunities to minimise transportation distances, improve logistics, and source materials more sustainably.

AI also assists in eco-friendly product design by analysing material properties and recommending alternatives with lower environmental impact. Predictive analytics enable manufacturers to forecast demand accurately, preventing overproduction and reducing both energy use and material waste.

Furthermore, AI technologies monitor greenhouse gas emissions throughout manufacturing stages, ensuring compliance with sustainability regulations and enabling corrective action when necessary. Additive manufacturing methods, such as AI-assisted 3D printing, further reduce waste by optimising material usage.

By integrating AI into every stage of production, manufacturers can lower emissions, cut costs, and achieve sustainability targets, contributing to a global shift towards low-carbon industrial practices.

Why AI is Key to Sustainable Water Management?

AI is becoming indispensable in managing water resources sustainably by optimising usage, monitoring quality, and reducing waste. Smart AI-powered sensors collect real-time data on water consumption, quality, and distribution, helping cities and industries manage resources more effectively.

Machine learning algorithms predict water demand patterns, ensuring that supply meets need without over-extraction or shortages. In agriculture, AI-driven irrigation systems analyse soil and weather data to deliver precise water volumes, significantly conserving this critical resource.

AI technologies detect leaks and inefficiencies in water distribution networks, enabling timely repairs and minimising water loss. In treatment plants, AI enhances filtration and purification processes, improving water quality while reducing energy usage.

Moreover, AI-powered storage management systems ensure optimal water availability during dry seasons, supporting resilience against droughts. AI also monitors pollution levels in rivers, lakes, and reservoirs, allowing for rapid response to contamination events.

When integrated into smart city infrastructures, AI coordinates water management alongside energy, transportation, and waste systems, contributing to a more sustainable urban ecosystem.

Why the Role of AI in Electric Vehicle (EV) Infrastructure?

AI is accelerating the global shift towards electric mobility by optimising the development and management of EV infrastructure. Machine learning algorithms analyse traffic patterns, population density, and driver behaviours to determine the best locations for EV charging stations, ensuring maximum accessibility and efficiency.

AI-driven systems manage power distribution intelligently, predicting charging demand and dynamically adjusting supply to reduce wait times and improve station performance. By continuously monitoring charging stations, AI detects faults and schedules maintenance proactively, minimising downtime and ensuring consistent availability.

In fleet management, AI enhances operational efficiency by optimising vehicle routes, charging schedules, and battery usage, reducing costs and energy consumption. Advanced battery management systems powered by AI predict battery health, optimise charging cycles, and extend battery lifespan.

Furthermore, AI integrates EV infrastructure with smart grids, balancing energy flows and preventing overload during peak demand hours. These systems also enable vehicle-to-grid (V2G) technologies, allowing EVs to supply excess stored energy back to the grid when idle.

By enabling smarter, more efficient EV networks, AI supports the mass adoption of sustainable transportation solutions, driving the global transition to cleaner mobility.

Why AI is Revolutionising Green Building Design?

AI is reshaping the future of green building design by enabling architects, engineers, and developers to create highly sustainable structures. AI-powered design tools analyse factors like natural lighting, ventilation, and insulation to develop energy-efficient building plans that minimise reliance on artificial heating, cooling, and lighting.

Machine learning models evaluate energy consumption patterns to help architects design buildings that remain efficient throughout their entire lifecycle. AI also supports the selection of sustainable materials by assessing environmental impact, durability, and local availability, promoting eco-friendly sourcing practices.

Additionally, AI optimises heating, ventilation, and air conditioning (HVAC) systems in real-time, ensuring they operate at peak efficiency while reducing energy waste. Predictive maintenance tools powered by AI identify potential equipment failures before they occur, prolonging system lifespan and lowering repair costs.

During construction, AI improves project planning, reducing material waste and optimising logistics for sustainable operations. Once completed, smart building technologies powered by AI monitor energy usage continuously and automatically adjust systems to maintain efficiency.

AI's integration into green building design enables the creation of eco-friendly, cost-effective, and sustainable spaces that align with long-term environmental goals.

Why the Future of AI in Green Tech: Innovation and Sustainability?

The future of AI in green technology promises to revolutionise global sustainability efforts. As industries adopt renewable energy, eco-friendly transportation, and circular economies, AI will act as a catalyst for innovation and efficiency.

Machine learning algorithms will continue optimising energy generation, distribution, and consumption across sectors, reducing waste and promoting environmental responsibility. Predictive maintenance and real-time monitoring powered by AI will make industrial systems more reliable, cost-effective, and sustainable.

In urban planning, AI will advance smart city ecosystems, integrating renewable energy sources, efficient transportation networks, and green infrastructure to reduce carbon footprints. AI-driven breakthroughs in energy storage, hydrogen fuel, and carbon capture technologies will make renewable solutions more scalable and affordable.

Furthermore, AI will foster cross-industry collaboration, uniting governments, private sectors, and communities in tackling climate change. Through its integration with the Internet of Things (IoT), AI will drive next-generation solutions in water, energy, and waste management, contributing to a cleaner, smarter planet.

AI will be at the core of future green innovations, helping humanity achieve environmental sustainability on a global scale.

Why AI's Role is Important in Advancing Environmental Conservation?

AI is transforming environmental conservation by providing advanced tools to monitor ecosystems, protect biodiversity, and manage natural resources sustainably. AI-powered monitoring systems track wildlife populations, detect poaching threats, and support data-driven conservation strategies.

Machine learning models analyse environmental data to identify early signs of habitat degradation, pollution, or climate change impacts, enabling timely interventions. AI-driven drones and satellite imagery offer real-time insights into forest health, water quality, and soil conditions, supporting more precise environmental assessments.

AI also optimises land-use planning by analysing ecological data to ensure natural resources are utilised responsibly while preserving fragile ecosystems. In climate research, AI predicts weather and climate patterns, improving disaster preparedness and supporting climate resilience efforts.

Additionally, AI aids in ecological restoration projects by optimising reforestation plans, coral reef rehabilitation, and habitat preservation strategies. By analysing large datasets, conservationists can target interventions more effectively and maximise impact.

Through its integration into environmental conservation, AI empowers humanity to safeguard biodiversity, mitigate climate change effects, and preserve ecosystems for future generations.

Chapter 11

Biotechnology

and Health

Why AI in Drug Discovery?

AI is revolutionising the drug discovery process by transforming how researchers analyse data, identify potential drug candidates, and bring life-saving medications to market. Traditionally, discovering new drugs has been a time-consuming and costly process, often taking years or even decades. However, with AI, these timelines are significantly reduced, sometimes from years to just a few months.

AI achieves this by analysing vast datasets, including chemical libraries, molecular structures, and clinical results, to predict molecular interactions. Machine learning models can pinpoint potential drug candidates much faster than traditional methods, allowing researchers to explore molecules that were previously overlooked.

Additionally, AI predicts possible side effects and optimises drug formulations before clinical trials begin. This helps in minimising risks, improving safety, and enhancing drug effectiveness. During urgent medical crises, such as pandemics, AI can assist in identifying existing drugs that can be repurposed to treat emerging diseases, thus accelerating response times.

By automating repetitive simulations and data-driven processes, AI enhances research efficiency and accuracy. It also identifies biomarkers that support precision medicine, enabling treatments to be more personalised. Since AI models continuously learn from new clinical data, future drug discovery efforts become increasingly refined and effective. The integration of AI with biotechnology opens the door to ground-breaking innovations, increasing the likelihood of discovering life-saving treatments and cures.

Why AI in Precision Medicine?

AI is transforming precision medicine by enabling highly personalised healthcare strategies that are tailored to each individual's genetic, environmental, and lifestyle factors. Unlike traditional 'one-size-fits-all' approaches, AI analyses complex datasets to predict how a patient will respond to specific therapies, resulting in more accurate and effective treatments.

Machine learning models identify genetic markers linked to various diseases, which allows doctors to make more precise diagnoses. AI also helps minimise trial-and-error prescribing by recommending the most suitable medications based on each patient's genetic profile.

Furthermore, AI-powered analytics continuously track patient progress and adapt treatment plans in real-time to maximise effectiveness. When combined with genomics, AI enables personalised solutions for complex diseases such as cancer, diabetes, and autoimmune disorders.

In the case of rare genetic conditions, AI identifies potential treatment options that traditional research methods might overlook. It also accelerates genome sequencing, making it faster and more affordable. By matching medications to a patient's unique biology, AI reduces side effects, improves healthcare outcomes, and enhances quality of life, while simultaneously reducing costs across the healthcare system.

Why AI in Early Disease Detection?

AI plays a pivotal role in early disease detection by analysing medical images, patient histories, and laboratory results to uncover subtle signs of illness long before symptoms appear.

In oncology, AI algorithms process X-rays, CT scans, and MRIs to identify the earliest signs of cancer, improving the chances of successful treatment. Similarly, AI detects biomarkers in blood tests to diagnose conditions such as diabetes, cardiovascular diseases, and kidney disorders earlier and more accurately.

AI also predicts the onset of neurological diseases like Alzheimer's and Parkinson's by analysing brain scans, genetic markers, and cognitive patterns. In cardiology, AI monitors heart rhythms to detect arrhythmias and other irregularities in real-time, helping prevent potentially life-threatening complications.

By identifying diseases at their pre-symptomatic stages, AI enables timely intervention and more effective treatment plans. It also improves the accuracy of routine screenings, reducing missed diagnoses and unnecessary medical expenses. This early, data-driven approach leads to better patient outcomes and overall healthcare efficiency.

Why AI in Genomic Medicine?

AI is redefining genomic medicine by accelerating the analysis and interpretation of complex genetic data. By studying vast amounts of genomic information, AI helps researchers diagnose genetic disorders, develop targeted therapies, and prevent diseases.

It identifies mutations linked to conditions like cystic fibrosis, sickle cell anaemia, and other inherited disorders, enabling earlier and more accurate diagnoses. AI also interprets large-scale genomic datasets to understand how specific genes contribute to disease development.

In the realm of precision medicine, AI designs more efficient gene therapies by predicting the outcomes of genetic modifications and selecting optimal approaches. AI-driven systems also discover new genes associated with diseases, leading to the creation of novel therapeutic targets.

By analysing DNA sequences, AI predicts how genetic variations may influence drug responses, helping doctors choose the safest and most effective treatments while reducing adverse reactions. AI also contributes to mapping the human genome, streamlining sequencing processes to make them faster and more affordable.

Through its ability to manage, process, and interpret massive volumes of data, AI drives advancements in genomic medicine, opening new frontiers for disease prevention, treatment, and personalised care.

Why AI in Clinical Trials?

AI is revolutionising clinical trials by streamlining every stage of the process, from patient recruitment to data analysis and reporting.

Machine learning algorithms scan electronic health records (EHR) to identify eligible patients, ensuring accurate matches between participants and trial requirements. AI also designs smarter trials by predicting which treatments are most likely to succeed based on patient characteristics and historical data.

By automating data collection, monitoring, and analysis, AI significantly reduces both time and costs. It enhances patient safety by detecting adverse effects in real-time and improving compliance with trial protocols. AI-driven systems also identify hidden patterns within large datasets, uncovering insights that traditional methods might miss.

Additionally, AI simplifies administrative tasks such as scheduling, data entry, and regulatory reporting, reducing human error and freeing researchers to focus on innovation. With predictive modelling, trial designs are optimised for higher success rates.

Overall, AI makes clinical trials more efficient, cost-effective, and data-driven, ultimately accelerating the delivery of ground-breaking therapies to patients.

Why AI in Healthcare Diagnostics?

AI is transforming healthcare diagnostics by improving accuracy, efficiency, and speed in detecting diseases.

AI-powered algorithms process medical images, including X-rays, MRIs, and CT scans, to detect conditions such as cancer, fractures, pneumonia, and other abnormalities with remarkable precision. In pathology, AI analyses tissue samples to identify early signs of diseases like cancer, while in cardiology, it interprets ECG signals to detect irregular heart rhythms.

AI diagnostic tools also analyse blood tests to uncover issues like high cholesterol, abnormal glucose levels, or deficiencies in immune markers. Over time, these systems learn and adapt, continuously improving diagnostic accuracy.

By integrating global databases of rare diseases and biomarkers, AI also assists in diagnosing conditions that are otherwise difficult to detect. This not only speeds up decision-making for healthcare providers but also ensures patients receive faster, more effective treatments.

AI's growing role in diagnostics reduces errors, enhances predictive capabilities, and ensures better patient outcomes through accurate, timely insights.

Why AI in Healthcare Administration?

AI is streamlining healthcare administration by automating time-consuming tasks and improving overall operational efficiency.

From scheduling patient appointments and managing hospital beds to processing billing and insurance claims, AI simplifies complex workflows. Predictive analytics optimise patient flow by identifying potential appointment cancellations and reallocating resources accordingly.

AI also assists in maintaining accurate electronic health records by identifying missing information and correcting discrepancies. Automating coding and billing reduces manual errors, speeds up claim approvals, and enhances financial efficiency.

AI-driven chatbots handle patient queries, appointment reminders, and administrative requests, improving patient engagement and satisfaction. Furthermore, AI predicts patient demand, helping hospitals manage staff schedules more effectively.

By automating repetitive tasks and optimising hospital resources, AI frees healthcare professionals to focus more on patient care while enhancing transparency and reducing operational costs.

Why AI in Medical Imaging?

AI is reshaping medical imaging by providing faster, more precise analyses of X-rays, MRIs, CT scans, and ultrasounds.

Deep learning algorithms detect subtle abnormalities in images that human radiologists may overlook, ensuring early and accurate disease detection.

For instance, AI identifies tumours, fractures, neurological conditions, and vascular issues with exceptional precision.

AI-assisted imaging tools significantly reduce waiting times for patients by accelerating diagnostic processes. In radiology, AI automatically flags urgent cases, enabling doctors to prioritise patients requiring immediate attention. It also helps in staging diseases such as cancer, aiding doctors in planning the most effective treatment strategies.

By reducing diagnostic errors and enhancing workflow efficiency, AI allows healthcare systems to handle larger volumes of imaging data without compromising quality. The integration of AI into imaging technologies makes healthcare faster, more accessible, and more reliable.

Why AI in Mental Health?

AI is making mental health care more personalised, accessible, and effective by providing tools for early detection, tailored treatment, and ongoing patient support.

AI-driven platforms analyse speech patterns, written communication, and facial expressions to detect early signs of conditions such as depression, anxiety, and PTSD. Virtual assistants powered by AI offer personalised cognitive behavioural therapy (CBT), emotional counselling, and stress management strategies through chatbots and apps.

AI-based monitoring systems track patients' mental health by observing mood changes, sleep patterns, and activity levels, adjusting treatment recommendations in real time. It also provides immediate coping strategies and relaxation techniques to manage symptoms as they arise.

By predicting patient needs and treatment responses, AI allows clinicians to deliver more effective care. It also improves accessibility by offering anonymous, stigma-free support, particularly for individuals in underserved or remote areas.

AI's data-driven approach is reshaping mental health services, empowering patients with continuous support while enabling healthcare professionals to provide better outcomes.

Why AI in Biomanufacturing?

AI is transforming biomanufacturing by enhancing production efficiency, improving quality control, and accelerating the development of life-saving therapies.

AI systems analyse large-scale production data to detect inefficiencies, optimise the use of raw materials, and reduce energy consumption. In vaccine production, AI streamlines formulation, testing, and approval processes, ensuring faster availability during public health emergencies.

By predicting biologic performance during manufacturing, AI reduces waste, increases yields, and ensures consistency in product quality. Real-time monitoring enables early identification of potential production issues, preventing costly delays.

AI also optimises cell culture conditions for monoclonal antibody production, allowing for large-scale manufacturing while maintaining safety and quality standards. With AI-based automation, biomanufacturing becomes more scalable, reliable, and cost-effective.

Furthermore, AI ensures compliance with regulatory standards by recording and analysing production data for audits. The integration of AI in biomanufacturing accelerates the delivery of innovative therapies and vaccines, making advanced treatments more widely available.

Conclusion

As we reach the end of this journey through the evolving landscape of innovation, one thing becomes abundantly clear: we are living in an era defined by possibility. From artificial intelligence and autonomous systems to quantum computing, biotechnology, and sustainable technologies, every breakthrough we've explored reflects humanity's relentless pursuit of progress.

The chapters of this book have taken us deep into the heart of transformation, uncovering the ***'why'*** behind the technologies shaping our world and our future. We have examined ***why AI drives efficiency***, ***why robotics redefines industries***, ***why sustainability is no longer optional***, and ***why exploring space opens the doors to***

unimaginable opportunities. Each ***'why'*** connects to a larger vision of innovation powered by curiosity, creativity, and a shared hope for a better tomorrow.

But this is not the end; it is an invitation. An invitation to keep questioning, to keep imagining, and to keep striving. Because behind every leap forward lies a simple yet powerful question: ***'Why not?'***

The future belongs to those who dare to ask, to learn, and to build. And as technology continues to blur the boundaries between the possible and the impossible, we find ourselves not just witnessing the future; we are shaping it.

So, let us move forward with open minds, bold ambitions, and the courage to innovate. The answers we seek today will spark the questions of tomorrow, and with each question, we will continue to redefine what it means to be human in an age of extraordinary change.

Profitable Pointers

- The **Future Belongs to Purpose-Driven AI**

  AI will not just be measured by *what* it can automate or *how* it scales, but by *why* it exists in the first place. Companies that embed AI with a **clear purpose**—improving human capability, decision-making, or societal outcomes—will dominate the future marketplace.

- Profit **Lies in Human–AI Symbiosis, Not Substitution**

  The most profitable AI systems will be those that **augment human intelligence**, not replace it. By asking *why* we want AI to handle a task, businesses can avoid blind automation and instead create tools that generate **new markets, better services, and deeper trust**.

- **"Why" Drives Trust, and Trust Drives Adoption**

  In the next decade, customers and regulators will demand explain ability. The organisations that can answer the *why* behind every algorithmic decision will win **trust, adoption, and sustainable profits**, while "black box" AI risks becoming obsolete.

- The **Why Code is the New Competitive Moat**

  Any company can adopt AI frameworks, but few can articulate the deeper *why*. Embedding ethical reasoning, responsible design, and long-term vision will act as a **strategic moat**, ensuring profits are not just immediate but resilient to disruption.

- Profits **Follow Meaningful Innovation**

  History shows that the most profitable innovations (internet, smartphones, cloud) were those that answered a fundamental *why*. In the AI era, the winners will be those who align **advanced intelligence with meaningful human needs**, not just technical capability.

The future belongs to purpose-driven AI. The businesses that articulate the "why" behind their AI adoption will not only gain competitive advantage but also secure lasting customer trust.

AI profits will come less from substitution and more from symbiosis. The companies that design AI to augment human intelligence, rather than replace it, will create entirely new markets and services.

Trust is the new currency. Explaining "why" an algorithm made a decision will be the defining factor in whether customers adopt or reject AI solutions

As you close these pages, remember: technology is not only about algorithms and code; it is about purpose. The future of AI will not be shaped by machines alone, but by the questions we dare to ask, and the why *that guides our journey forward.*

Technology can compute, but only humans can question. The future of AI will be written not by code alone, but by the why *that fuels our vision and purpose.*

Index

A

B

C

G

H

I

L

M

N

P

Q

R

S

www.ingramcontent.com/pod-product-compliance
Lightning Source LLC
LaVergne TN
LVHW052113210926
848482LV00025B/580